DONALD TRUMP IN HISTORICAL PERSPECTIVE

Donald Trump in Historical Perspective is a collection of chapters that utilizes the thinking of historians, philosophers, and political scientists to explore historical parallels to the presidency of Donald J. Trump, the 45th President of the United States of America.

This collection provides an extensive analysis on the ways Trump's impulsiveness, breaking of norms, and disregard for long-standing democratic pieties, caused him to represent a definitive end to the "American century," an era when American self confidence, steadiness, and leadership, even in the face of titanic challenges, were almost universally taken for granted. Yet this book also argues how in the longer sweep of history, Trump is a familiar figure in the turbulent life of democracies. These in-depth chapters reveal the ways Trump represents the anti-institutionalist, the populist demagogue, the would-be authoritarian who exploits electoral and political vulnerabilities to gain and hold power. Through these detailed evaluations, these chapters suggest that Trump is not radically unique but that democracies have produced many previous versions of the Trump phenomenon.

This book is essential reading for scholars and students in political science, political theory, history, and leadership. This book is also noteworthy for readers interested in key developments in contemporary American democracy. One of its greatest appeals is its extensive look into leadership on an international scale, from Donald Trump's global significance to various explorations of non-American leaders, and the comparisons that can be made.

Michael Harvey is Provost and Dean, Washington College in Chestertown, Maryland.

Leadership: Research and Practice Series

Series Editor
Ronald E. Riggio, Henry R. Kravis
Professor of Leadership and Organizational Psychology and former Director of the Kravis Leadership Institute at Claremont McKenna College

In Memoriam
Georgia Sorenson (1947–2020), Founding Editor

Inclusive Leadership
Transforming Diverse Lives, Workplaces, and Societies
Edited by Bernardo M. Ferdman, Jeanine Prime, and Ronald E. Riggio

Leadership Across Boundaries
A Passage to Aporia
Nathan Harter

A Theory of Environmental Leadership
Leading for the Earth
Mark Manolopoulos

Handbook of International and Cross-Cultural Leadership Research Processes
Perspectives, Practice, Instruction
Yulia Tolstikov-Mast, Franziska Bieri, and Jennie L. Walker

Deepening the Leadership Journey
Nine Elements of Leadership Mastery
Al Bolea and Leanne Atwater

Donald Trump in Historical Perspective
Dead Precedents
Edited by Michael Harvey

For more information about this series, please visit: www.routledge.com/Leadership-Research-and-Practice/book-series/leadership

DONALD TRUMP IN HISTORICAL PERSPECTIVE

Dead Precedents

Edited by Michael Harvey

Routledge
Taylor & Francis Group
NEW YORK AND LONDON

First published 2022
by Routledge
605 Third Avenue, New York, NY 10158

and by Routledge
4 Park Square, Milton Park, Abingdon, Oxon OX14 4RN

Routledge is an imprint of the Taylor & Francis Group, an informa business

Library of Congress Cataloging-in-Publication Data
A catalog record for this book has been requested

ISBN: 978-0-367-62697-6 (hbk)
ISBN: 978-0-367-62695-2 (pbk)
ISBN: 978-1-003-11036-1 (ebk)

DOI: 10.4324/9781003110361

Typeset in Bembo
by Apex CoVantage, LLC

CONTENTS

SERIES FOREWORD

As a leadership scholar, I (along with my colleagues) watched that Donald Trump, a man with no political experience and little leadership experience (except for running an inherited real estate enterprise), became the leader of the most powerful nation on earth. What followed was a display of some of the very worst forms of leadership—sowing divisions instead of unity, straining international relations with allies, vilifying immigrants and marginalized citizens, and mishandling a raging epidemic. During all of this, his supporters grew more devoted to him, while his opponents were dismayed. I remember waking up each morning with trepidation reading Trump's latest outrageous tweet.

As experts on leadership, we watched that President Donald Trump seemed to defy all forms of logic and proven leadership practices while ineptly steering the country. Those of us who study leadership with the intention of improving leadership practices worldwide began to think that Donald Trump had "rewritten" the book on bad leadership. What this volume tells us is that history can indeed repeat itself and that past eras have seen their share of unscrupulous and dangerous leaders. By reading these accounts of past leaders, and comparing them to former President Trump, we can indeed improve leadership worldwide by not falling prey to such leaders in the future. In short, through studying bad leaders, we should learn to avoid them. For those of us who are students of leadership, and for seated leaders, this book provides an important guide for keeping leaders on the right path.

Ronald E. Riggio

CONTRIBUTORS

Mallory Monaco Caterine is Senior Professor of Practice, Department of Classical Studies, Tulane University. Professor Monaco Caterine earned her Ph.D. at Princeton University, writing a dissertation on the significance of the Hellenistic past in Plutarch's Lives. Her research and teaching interests include post-classical Greek cultural history and prose literature and leadership in the ancient world, with a focus on tyrants and women. She has co-organized two online ancient leadership syllabi as well as an online conference on the teaching of leaders and leadership through Classics and continues to promote a humanistic approach to leadership education inside and outside of academia.

Simonetta Falasca-Zamponi is Professor of Sociology at the University of California, Santa Barbara, where she teaches course in social theory and cultural analysis. She is the author of *Fascist Spectacle: The Aesthetics of Power in Mussolini's Italy* and of numerous other works on the relationship between politics and culture.

Michael Harvey is Provost and Dean, Washington College (Chestertown, Maryland). He is the co-editor, with Professor Ronald E. Riggio of Claremont College, of *Leadership Studies: The Dialogue of Disciplines*, published by Edward Elgar in 2011. He is the author of *The Nuts and Bolts of College Writing* (2003, third edition 2020).

Mark A. Menaldo is Associate Professor of Political Science and Director of the School of Liberal Arts at Texas A&M University-Commerce. He earned his Ph.D. from Michigan State University in 2010. In 2013, his book *Leadership and Transformative Ambition in International Relations* was published in the New Horizons in Leadership Studies from Edward Elgar Publishing. He is the co-editor with Brent Cusher of a 2018 book, *Leadership and the Unmasking of*

Authenticity: The Philosophy of Self-Knowledge and Deception, also published by Edward Elgar.

J.M. Opal is Associate Professor and Chair, Department of History, McGill University. Jason M. Opal studies colonial North America, the American Revolution, and the early decades of the United States. His work tries to integrate social, cultural, and intellectual history and to shed light on broad topics such as nationalism, capitalism, and democracy. Opal did his undergraduate work at Cornell and his doctoral studies at Brandeis, where he worked with historians such as Jane Kamensky, David Hackett Fischer, and James T. Kloppenberg. His first major project was on the cultural transformation of ambition in the post-Revolutionary New England countryside. It resulted in an article in the *Journal of American History* in 2004 that won the Organization of American Historians' Binkley-Stephenson Award and, in the 2008 book, *Beyond the Farm: National Ambitions in Rural New England*, published by the University of Pennsylvania Press. His second project focused on the southern borderlands of the American Revolution and the rise of Andrew Jackson as the leader of an American national concept joining modern property regimes and epic religious narratives. Supported by a Social Sciences and Humanities Research Council grant, this research culminated in the 2017 book, *Avenging the People: Andrew Jackson, the Rule of Law, and the American Nation* by Oxford University Press. This book was chosen by the History Book Club and the Military History Book Club in the United States and selected as one of the "best summer books" in history and law by *The Times* of London. His recent writings have also appeared in *The Washington Post*, The *Los Angeles Times*, Salon, The Walrus, The Conversation, and Jacobin. His new projects are Most Noble Island: Three Ages of Barbados in the Early Americas and a collaborative project with his father, Dr. Steven M. Opal, on the history of epidemic diseases in American life. At McGill, Opal teaches surveys of the early United States and the American Revolution as well as more specialized courses on the history of slavery, US foreign relations, democracy, and the family.

Bin Song is Assistant Professor of Philosophy and Religion at Washington College. He earned his Ph.D. in Religious Studies from Boston University in 2018. A scholar of Ruism (Confucianism), his publications have appeared in both English and Chinese journals.

Sarah Thelen received her Ph.D. in History from American University (Washington, DC) and has been an Instructional Designer with the Office of the Vice-President for Teaching and Learning at University College Cork (Ireland) since January 2013. She has taught graduate and undergraduate modules at universities in the United States and Ireland, worked at the Nixon Presidential Library (US National Archives and Records Administration), and published articles on President Richard Nixon in the *Journal of American Studies* and *49th Parallel.*

Alfonso Vergaray is Assistant Professor of International Leadership at Texas A&M International University.

1

INTRODUCTION

History's Rhymes

Michael Harvey

> The instability, injustice, and confusion introduced into the public councils, have in truth been the mortal diseases under which popular governments have everywhere perished.
>
> *(Federalist 10)*

> Just say the election was corrupt + leave the rest to me and the R[epublican] congressmen.
>
> *(Donald Trump, December 2020)*[1]

On the evening of November 8, 1923, Adolph Hitler attempted a coup d'état to overthrow Germany's Weimar Republic. Two thousand members of the Nazi party, several hundred of them armed Brownshirt paramilitaries, marched to a large beer hall in Munich, in the southeastern German state of Bavaria, where Gustav Ritter von Kahr, part of a ruling triumvirate with emergency powers in Bavaria, a state in southeastern Germany, was making a speech. Hitler hoped that a dramatic show of force would be enough to let him seize power. His Brownshirts surrounded the hall and set up a heavy machine gun inside. Over several hours, Hitler fired his pistol into the ceiling, delivered passionate oratory, negotiated frantically with Kahr and the other two members of the triumvirate (general Otto von Lossow and police chief Hans Ritter von Seisser), and used all his energy to win over the audience. He argued that Germany faced an emergency, that traitors were working to destroy the nation, and that supporting him was the patriotic thing to do. Ordinary Germans, like those in the hall, had the power to save the country. He urged his audience to compel the emergency triumvirate to endorse his leadership:

> Outside are Kahr, Lossow, and Seisser. They are struggling hard to reach a decision. May I say to them that you will stand behind them? . . . I

DOI: 10.4324/9781003110361-1

> can say this to you: Either the German revolution begins tonight or we will all be dead by dawn![2]

Hitler won the moment, the crowd erupting in cheers and the three men pledging their support. But the coup attempt quickly dissipated, and within a few months Hitler was in jail, where he would sit for eight months before being released. Still, the abortive coup helped rather than hurt Hitler's political career. Inspired in part by Mussolini's March on Rome the previous year, the Beer Hall Putsch had less immediate impact but increased Hitler's celebrity. He used his time in jail to write *Mein Kampf*, which sold well and brought his message of fascistic grievance populism to a much larger audience. He also decided to compete politically mostly within legal bounds—a strategic choice that paid off a decade later, when Adolf Hitler, one of humanity's most malevolent and destructive tyrants, gained power by democratic and legal means.

History may not repeat itself, but it rhymes, especially when it comes to one of the oldest patterns in human communities: a would-be strong man's attempt to seize power by exploiting a dramatic moment and claiming to be the savior of a community in danger. Niccolò Machiavelli's writings, for instance, are full of such figures, from the ancient tyrant Agathocles of Syracuse to the 15th-century Oliverotto da Fermo: they are part of a long parade in Machiavelli's writings, and indeed in history, of restless, ambitious, energetic men seizing the moment, standing on stages or riding on horseback, unleashing violence, spilling blood, delivering stirring words, and usually falling short—but sometimes succeeding in the desperate bid for power.

Consider one such instance: the storming of the Capitol in Washington, DC, on January 6, 2021. January 6 is the day established by US law for a joint session of Congress to receive and count the votes of the Electoral College, the final step in a solemn bureaucratic chain of state gatherings, votes, and certifications that serve to translate November's national election into January's peaceful transition of power. Normally this is a pro forma series of meetings and actions. But Donald Trump, the outgoing president, perceived that his sole chance to retain power lay in upending the process. After the election, for weeks, he put pressure on the individual men and women charged with responsibility and action at every step: state officials responsible for certifying election results, governors, members of Congress, and his own vice-president.[3] He claimed the election had been stolen from him and urged his followers to take action to "stop the steal." He pushed his team of advisors to develop arguments to support his claim. He planned a national rally—the March to Save America—to put pressure on Congress on the last possible day. And, for weeks, he urged his supporters to attend the rally, as in this tweet from December 19, 2020: "Big protest in D.C. on January 6th. Be there, will be wild!"[4] On the morning of January 6, he summed up the specious case for overturning the election in a tweet to his 88 million followers:

> States want to correct their votes, which they now know were based on irregularities and fraud, plus corrupt process never received legislative

> approval. All Mike Pence has to do is send them back to the States, AND WE WIN. Do it Mike, this is a time for extreme courage![5]

At noon on January 6, on a stage that he had prepared just south of the grounds of the White House, on the open field facing the Washington Monument, Trump spoke to his supporters. As with the Beer Hall Putsch, a would-be leader tried to take advantage of an already scheduled event (in Hitler's case, Kahr's speech; in Trump's, Congress's tallying of the electoral votes) to create a dramatic moment with himself at the center of attention, calling for bold action to upend the political order. Unlike Hitler's coup attempt, Trump already held top office, so he was attempting to hold onto power, not seize it (the precise term for Trump's intended action is a 'self-coup' or 'autogolpe'). Thus, Trump was able to plan for the event well in advance, and with much greater control, including developing the legal arguments that could be used to justify rejecting the election's results.[6]

Just as Hitler had asked his audience to put pressure on the three leaders in Bavaria "struggling hard to reach a decision," Trump asked his supporters to put pressure on the members of Congress gathered a mile away:

> Mike Pence is going to have to come through for us. . . . it is up to Congress to confront this egregious assault on our democracy. And after this, we're going to walk down, and I'll be there with you, we're going to walk down. . . . we're going to walk down to the Capitol, and we're going to cheer on our brave senators and congressmen and women, and we're probably not going to be cheering so much for some of them. Because you'll never take back our country with weakness. You have to show strength and you have to be strong. We have come to demand that Congress do the right thing and only count the electors who have been lawfully slated, lawfully slated. I know that everyone here will soon be marching over to the Capitol building to peacefully and patriotically make your voices heard.[7]

None of this, of course, is an explicit call to violence; to be fair to Trump, he didn't bring a machine gun or a pistol to the event, and indeed he emphasized taking action "peacefully." Nor did he even live up to his own words—he did not walk with his supporters to the Capitol, but watched events unfold on TV in the White House. But as with the Beer Hall Putsch, the man at the center of the action made a florid, emotional case that a political crisis existed, and required immediate action by patriots; there was an attempt to overawe with violence and a show of force; there were clashes between police officers and zealous partisans; and, in both abortive attempts, people died—20 demonstrators and police in the case of the Beer Hall Putsch, five demonstrators and police in the case of the storming of the Capitol. And that does not count the four police officers who committed suicide in subsequent months, as Trump and his minions assailed them across social media for anti-democratic treachery, corruption, and murder.[8]

Nine months after January 6 Trump released a video commemorating the birthday of Ashli Babbitt, who was shot and killed trying to breach a room where members of Congress were hiding from the mob:

> To Ashli's family and friends, please know that her memory will live on in our hearts for all time. . . . There was no reason Ashli should've lost her life that day. We must all demand justice for Ashli and her family, so on this solemn occasion as we celebrate her life, we renew our call for a fair and nonpartisan investigation into the death of Ashli Babbitt.[9]

Just as the Beer Hall Putsch became, in the busy hands of Nazi propagandists, a bedrock of the legend of Adolf Hitler and a driver of his subsequent rise to power, the events of January 6 have become, for millions of Americans, a defining story of patriotism and direct action that will lead, if justice prevails, to the restoration of Donald Trump to his rightful place—President of the United States.

⋆ ⋆ ⋆

This is a book of historical comparisons to the extraordinary presidency of Donald Trump. Trump is a startling and disorienting figure in American political culture—the demagogue who gets elected president and then sets out to undermine, overturn, and destroy the system of elections itself. But while Trump's achievement is new in American politics, it is familiar on the world stage. Indeed, the ancient Greeks recognized that democracy and demagogues go together, so this book starts the comparisons there. We begin with Plutarch, the 1st-century Greek biographer and writer, whose comparisons of prominent figures from Greece and Rome established comparative detailed study of a 'life' as a significant part of leadership studies. Plutarch's comparisons allow detailed study of one life, matched to another in a different setting, to highlight differences and similarities. This book begins with a chapter on Plutarch himself and his approach to the study of individual leaders. Mallory Monaco Caterine introduces Plutarch's method, notes Plutarch's immense influence, including in American political thought, and suggests how the study of the past is part of the civic project of strengthening democracy. After this introduction to Plutarch, two chapters draw comparisons from the ancient world—Cleon of Athens, explored by Mark A. Menaldo, and Plato on the tyrannical soul, by Alfonso Vergaray. We then move to an early modern comparison, and Machiavelli's treatment of Trump-like figures like the Duke of Athens, seeking to grasp and hold onto power through adroit use of political theater.

The book then moves closer to the present, to an American comparison—the first truly populist president, Andrew Jackson, in a chapter by Jason Opal, who explores the many resonances—and some critical differences—between Jackson and Trump. Attention then turns to two international comparisons, Italy's Mussolini and China's Mao. Simonetta Falasca-Zamponi explores Mussolini's rise as tied to the development of celebrity and popular interest in politics as a parade of interesting personalities. And Bin Song explores the unexpected resonance between Donald Trump and Mao Zedong—both sought to anchor their populism in an approach characterized best as religious anti-intellectualism, as a way to sidestep established bureaucratic elites and connect directly with the people. The book's last comparison is to the most ignominious of American presidents, Richard Nixon. Sarah Thelen explores how Nixon, like Trump, built his appeal explicitly on racial appeals to a core of white nationalist supporters.

This historical context, ranging widely from ancient Greece to 20th-century China and America, helps us step back and look at the Trump phenomenon with some perspective. One rueful observation is that popular governments are inherently unstable. This was, for a very long time, part of the conventional wisdom about democracies: that they could work for a while, in some places, but that they were simply too unstable to endure, or to serve as a common model for decision-making, governance, and survival. Part of the instability came from their inherent limitation—if a state expanded, it was impossible for it to maintain the shared civic understandings that made democracy possible. Thus, Jean-Jacques Rousseau dedicated his *Discourse on Inequality* to the republic of Geneva, a city-state that he saw as the perfect size to endure as a democratic polity, for in a single city the people and the legislators could interact and know each other. The great example of democracy from the ancient world was the geographically limited polis—Athens, preeminently, where familiarity allowed citizens to understand themselves as engaged in a common project, with shared values. And even at this small scale, there was virtually no model in world history of a stable, enduring democracy. All democratic regimes, of whatever size, had quickly been overcome by tumult, or weakness, or corruption, or the rise of a demagogue who seized power and brought an end to the democratic experiment. This last, Alexander Hamilton, in the very first Federalist essay, conceded, was the most common way that democratic regimes died: "of those men who have overturned the liberties of republics, the greatest number have begun their career by paying an obsequious court to the people; commencing demagogues, and ending tyrants."[10]

From ancient to modern times, that has been the most common fate of democracies. The conviction that a democracy could endure, or could extend much beyond a city's walls, was a startling new claim, largely invented in America. The founders of the American republic took pains to acknowledge, in texts like the Federalist Papers, that while democracy was indeed fragile, they believed that due attention to the right structure, the right mechanical principle, and the right scale—the bigger the better—could turn democracies' weaknesses into strengths. Size alone, men such as Hamilton and Madison argued, reduced the risk of a demagogue rising to power:

> Extend the sphere, and you take in a greater variety of parties and interests; you make it less probable that a majority of the whole will have a common motive to invade the rights of other citizens. . . . The influence of factious leaders may kindle a flame within their particular States, but will be unable to spread a general conflagration through the other States.[11]

"In the extent and proper structure of the Union, therefore," Madison confidently concluded in Federalist 10, "we behold a republican remedy for the diseases most incident to republican government."

That "republican remedy" requires a critical element: a citizenry and a body of representatives that share sufficient epistemological ground that they can discuss, argue, and govern by wrestling with facts and opinions. A functioning democracy can be understood, from this perspective, as making possible "government by discussion," to use the famous phrase coined by the 19th-century English political thinker Walter Bagehot. What can threaten "government by discussion"? The rise not simply of political disagreement and partisan clash but also of severe epistemological disagreement that erodes trust, spreads fantasies of conspiracy, and undermines faith that normal political process will produce legitimate outcomes. When the normal machinery of "government by discussion" is no longer accepted by a sizable faction, "republican remedies" may cease to work. Alexander Hamilton, in a letter to George Washington in 1792, fretting over the ascendant political career of Aaron Burr, wrote, "the only path to a subversion of the republican system of the Country is, by flattering the prejudices of the people, and exciting their jealousies and apprehensions, to throw affairs into confusion, and bring on civil commotion."[12]

The Beer Hall Putsch of 1923 failed. It seemed at the time that the Weimar Republic had withstood Hitler's attempt do precisely what Hamilton had warned against in 1792. But the failure of the Putsch was just a temporary setback. Indeed, the failed attempt to seize power was something Hitler learned from, as the most respected historian of the Putsch concludes:

> He turned his attention towards preparing for the long haul. He built a more effective party machinery. He reorganized the shattered SA and the debilitated propaganda machine. He spread his version of the Putsch—and he waited for new crises that he was sure would come and lift him to power.[13]

What about the American Putsch? In the days following the assault on the Capitol by Trump's zealous partisans, a wave of revulsion and anger swept the country. The revulsion crossed party lines, so that January 6 seemed to mark the end of Donald Trump's political career: a last awful crescendo of violence and vicious hostility to democracy, rejected by the American people. The final verdict, it seemed, came from a most unlikely and significant source: Mitch McConnell, the Republican Senate majority leader. McConnell spoke on the floor of the Senate a month after the events of January 6, in a speech of such harrowing specificity and denunciatory power that it is necessary to quote it at length:

> January 6th was a disgrace. American citizens attacked their own government. . . . They stormed the Senate floor. They tried to hunt down the Speaker of the House. They built a gallows and chanted about murdering the Vice President. They did this because they had been fed wild falsehoods by the most powerful man on Earth—because he was angry he'd lost an election. Former President Trump's actions preceding the riot were a disgraceful dereliction of duty. . . .
>
> There is no question that President Trump is practically and morally responsible for provoking the events of that day. The people who stormed this building believed they were acting on the wishes and instructions of their President. And their having that belief was a foreseeable consequence of the growing crescendo of false statements, conspiracy theories, and reckless hyperbole which the defeated President kept shouting into the largest megaphone on planet Earth. . . . The leader of the free world cannot spend weeks thundering that shadowy forces are stealing our country and then feign surprise when people believe him and do reckless things. . . . This was an intensifying crescendo of conspiracy theories, orchestrated by an outgoing president who seemed determined to either overturn the voters' decision or else torch our institutions on the way out.
>
> The unconscionable behavior did not end when the violence began. Whatever our ex-President claims he thought might happen that day—whatever reaction he says he meant to produce—by that afternoon, he was watching the same live television as the rest of the world.
>
> A mob was assaulting the Capitol in his name. These criminals were carrying his banners, hanging his flags, and screaming their loyalty to him. It was obvious that only President Trump could end this. Former aides publicly begged him to do so. Loyal allies frantically called the Administration. But the President did not act swiftly. He did not do his job. He didn't take steps so federal law could be faithfully executed, and order restored. Instead, according to public reports, he watched television happily as the chaos unfolded. He kept pressing his scheme to overturn the election!
>
> Even after it was clear to any reasonable observer that Vice President Pence was in danger . . . even as the mob carrying Trump banners was beating cops and breaching perimeters . . . the President sent a further

> tweet attacking his Vice President. Predictably and foreseeably under the circumstances, members of the mob seemed to interpret this as further inspiration to lawlessness and violence. Later, even when the President did halfheartedly begin calling for peace, he did not call right away for the riot to end. He did not tell the mob to depart until even later. And even then, with police officers bleeding and broken glass covering Capitol floors, he kept repeating election lies and praising the criminals.[14]

But it must be noted that the same man who spoke these words voted to acquit Donald Trump of impeachment on that very day, on the floor of the Senate. When it came to what mattered—the real power of a vote that would conclusively end Trump's career—even McConnell dared not reject Trump. And, as days turn into weeks and months, it is clear that Trump's big lie about election fraud and a stolen election has become a bedrock doctrine among millions of his followers, and that a majority of Republicans now believe in the myth of the stolen election. According to a CNN poll in September 2021, eight months after January 6, almost 80% of Republicans believe Donald Trump, not Joe Biden, truly won the presidential election of 2020.[15]

The growth of the 'stolen election' lie is an ongoing political project: supported and spread by millions of ordinary Americans; sharpened to a point by a small army of strategists and loyalists; and originating, ultimately, from Trump himself, as in this speech to a group of aids and acolytes in November 2020, shortly after the election:

> People have got to know that this was stolen. This was taken from us. It was organized. And it wasn't even a close election. It was a fabrication. We won by a landslide. A landslide—and it was taken. This is what people need to understand—it was a landslide.[16]

The impact of Trump's big lie is felt in a thousand places, in a thousand small events—as in Texas, in October 2021, where a veteran non-partisan elections administrator, Michele Carew, resigned after months of hostility, vituperation, and social media attacks by both regular citizens and government officials. Her attackers seek to replace her non-partisan position with an elected official, with her likely replacement a "county clerk who has used social media to promote baseless allegations of widespread election fraud." Reflecting on her experience, Carew says, "When I started out, election administrators were appreciated and highly respected. Now we are made out to be the bad guys."[17]

Plutarch himself would most likely reject a "parallel lives" comparison of Adolf Hitler and Donald Trump. And of course there is no real comparison to be made of their lives and careers in full. Hitler's evil is incomparable—by the time he died, he had led the German people to exterminate two of every three Jews in Europe—six million men, women, and children in all—as well as millions of other civilians, and brought about the deaths of tens of millions of combatants in a ruinous global war. The most serious charge that can be leveled at Donald Trump is a grave one but still an order of magnitude less than Hitler: that Trump's feckless leadership is responsible for the needless deaths of hundreds of thousands of Americans in the Covid-19 pandemic.[18] Nevertheless, a comparison remains: in their impact on the democracies that elected each to national office. These are the two men in their two countries—Hitler in Germany and Trump in the United States—who did the most to destroy civic trust, weaken the state, and lie their way to power. Both men must be regarded as experts in using the everyday machinery of democracy—speeches, argument, rhetoric, partisanship, and elections—all the elements of "government by discussion"—to subvert and endanger democracy. Hitler's story is done. Trump's is not. It remains to be seen what the lessons of January 6, 2021, will be for Donald Trump, his followers, and America. To help us make sense of what has occurred, and what might come, what follows are some comparative explorations of the still-unfolding story of Donald Trump and the American people.

Notes

1 Dan Balz, "'Leave the Rest to Me': New DOJ Memos Show There's More to Learn about Trump and Jan. 6," *Washington Post*, July 31, 2021, www.washingtonpost.com/politics/leave-the-rest-to-me-new-doj-memos-show-theres-more-to-learn-about-trump-and-jan-6/2021/07/31/086cad9c-f185-11eb-a452-4da5fe48582d_story.html.

2 Ian Kershaw, *Hitler 1889–1936: Hubris* (New York: W. W. Norton, 1999), 297.

3 "You don't know the position I'm in," Vice-President Mike Pence whinged to a former vice-president, Dan Quayle, after weeks of brow-beating by Trump. Quayle, to his credit, was unsympathetic and urged Pence to do his duty: "I do know the position you're in. . . . I also know what the law is. You listen to the parliamentarian. That's all you do. You have no power" (Bob Woodward and Mike Costa, *Peril* (New York: Simon & Schuster, 2021)).

4 Dan Barry and Sheera Frenkel, "'Be There. Will Be Wild!': Trump All But Circled the Date," *New York Times*, January 6, 2021.

5 Danielle Rindler, "How One of America's Ugliest Days Unraveled Inside and Outside the Capitol," *Washington Post*, January 9, 2021.

6 Charles Davis, "Conservative Lawyer Penned 6-page Memo on How Mike Pence Could Hand the 2020 Election to Trump," *Business Insider*, September 21, 2021, www.businessinsider.com/memo-details-how-pence-could-hand-election-to-trump-exclusive-2021-9. A sample of the reasoning and argument in the memo, written by James Eastman and shared with members of Congress, in an effort to persuade them to support Trump's autogolpe:

> VP Pence opens the ballots, determines on his own which is valid, asserting that the authority to make that determination under the 12th Amendment, and the Adams and Jefferson precedents, is his alone (anything in the Electoral Count Act to the contrary is therefore unconstitutional). . . . If State Legislatures have not certified their own slates of electors, VP Pence determines, based on all the

> evidence and the letters from state legislators calling into question the executive certifications, decides to count neither slate of electors . . . At the end of the count, the tally would therefore be 232 for Trump, 222 for Biden. Because the 12th Amendment says "majority of electors *appointed*," having determined that no electors from the 7 states were appointed (a position in accord with that taken by Harvard Law Professor Laurence Tribe, TRUMP WINS.

7 "Trump's Jan. 6 Speech, A Key Part of Impeachment Trial," *NPR*, February 10, 2021, www.npr.org/2021/02/10/966396848/read-trumps-jan-6-speech-a-key-part-of-impeachment-trial.
8 Chelsey Cox and Matthew Brown, "Two Additional DC Officers Who Responded to U.S. Capitol Insurrection Die by Suicide," *USA Today*, August 2, 2021.
9 Zeeshan Aleem, "Trump's Ashli Babbitt Birthday Video Shows How He Hopes to Create a Martyr Out of Her," *MSNBC*, October 11, 2021, www.msnbc.com/opinion/trump-s-ashli-babbitt-birthday-video-shows-how-he-hopes-n1281255.
10 Alexander Hamilton, *Federalist* 1 (1787), https://billofrightsinstitute.org/activities/federalist-no-1-excerpts-annotated.
11 James Madison, *Federalist* 10 (1787), https://billofrightsinstitute.org/primary-sources/federalist-no-10.
12 Alexander Hamilton, *Letter to George Washington*, August 18, 1792, https://founders.archives.gov/documents/Hamilton/01-12-02-0184-0002#ARHN-01-12-02-0184-0002-fn-0005-ptr.
13 Harold J. Gordon, Jr., *Hitler and the Beer Hall Putsch* (Princeton, NJ: Princeton University Press, 1972), 618.
14 CNN, "Read McConnell's Remarks on the Senate Floor Following Trump's Acquittal," *CNN*, February 13, 2021, www.cnn.com/2021/02/13/politics/mcconnell-remarks-trump-acquittal/index.html.
15 Jennifer Agiesta and Ariel Edwards-Levy, "CNN Poll: Most Americans Feel Democracy is under Attack in the US," *CNN*, September 15, 2021, www.cnn.com/2021/09/15/politics/cnn-poll-most-americans-democracy-under-attack/index.html.
16 Michael Wolff, *Landslide: The Final Days of the Trump Presidency* (New York: Henry Holt and Company, 2021), 116.
17 Jeremy Schwartz, "Trump won Hood County in a Landslide. His Supporters Still Hounded the Elections," *Texas Tribune/Propublica*, October 12, 2021, www.texastribune.org/2021/10/12/hood-county-elections-administrator-trump/.
18 John Haltiwanger and Aylin Woodward, "Damning Analysis of Trump's Pandemic Response Suggested 40% of US COVID-19 Deaths Could Have Been Avoided," *Business Insider*, February 11, 2021, www.businessinsider.com/analysis-trump-covid-19-response-40-percent-us-deaths-avoidable-2021-2.

2

PLUTARCH AND THE PRECEDENTS FOR *DEAD PRECEDENTS*

Mallory Monaco Caterine

Dead Precedents is inspired by Plutarch, the Greek biographer of the 1st and 2nd centuries CE. But what does it mean to be "inspired by Plutarch"? In order to understand our source of inspiration, I outline key details of Plutarch's life, his historical context, and his literary output. Regarding the latter, our primary focus will be on Plutarch's biographical *magnum opus*, the *Parallel Lives*. We will consider his choice of subjects, distinctive features of his narrative style, and the consequences of his pioneering choice to write biographies in pairs. As will become clear, the form and composition of *Dead Precedents* depart quite dramatically from its Plutarchan inspiration. However, that departure puts the present volume in good company: Plutarch has long been used as a metonym for a range of ideas about biography, and I survey how that inspiration has manifested in a selection of American biographical works from the 1800s through the 21st century. Finally, I suggest what of Plutarch's spirit remains in *Dead Precedents* and discuss why these Plutarchan qualities are particularly well suited to making sense of the presidency of Donald Trump.

Plutarch of Chaeronea (c. 46–120 CE) was a philosopher, biographer, and local civic leader in the Roman province of Achaea (modern-day Greece). He was born into a prominent aristocratic family and sought to fulfill the obligations to his community attached to that position. As a young man, he witnessed the tumultuous reign of the Roman emperor Nero and the upheavals of 69 CE, the so-called "Year of the Four Emperors", which began with the fall of Nero and ended in the accession of Vespasian, the first emperor of the Flavian dynasty. The first dynastic change of the Roman Imperial period, this dramatic historical moment was marked by a dangerous, narcissistic tyrant, competing charismatic leaders, and ultimately, a competent, even-headed pragmatist

DOI: 10.4324/9781003110361-2

gaining power. The Flavian dynasty was short-lived, however, and fell in 96 CE when the emperor Domitian was assassinated by members of his own imperial court. Plutarch, around age 50 at this time, would have been at his political and intellectual prime. He held local offices, traveled to Rome on embassies, and was already establishing himself as a prominent intellectual figure. He had begun writing the *Moralia*, or *Moral Essays*, a diverse collection of philosophical and rhetorical treatises. When Domitian fell, the elderly and mild senator Nerva was acclaimed emperor. Nerva soon used the Roman tradition of adult adoption to designate Trajan, a successful and philanthropic general, as his heir; at Nerva's death in 99 CE, Trajan became emperor. After the trauma of Domitian's reign, in which the paranoid ruler regularly attacked any political men of prominence perceived to be a threat to his standing, members of the senatorial elite in Rome, such as Pliny the Younger, Suetonius, and Tacitus breathed a cautious sign of relief, hopeful that the new dynasty would be an era "when one can think what one likes and say what one thinks" (Tacitus, *Histories* 1.1). Overall, the historical record indicates that Nerva and Trajan's reigns did confirm their expectations of a return to civility, stability, and prosperity for the Roman Empire.

As a citizen of provincial Greece, Plutarch may not have felt the same existential threat from Domitian as his Roman contemporaries. That said, his literary output does indicate a similar sense of renewed freedom of speech, since it is after the accession of Nerva that Plutarch undertakes writing political biography in earnest. His first project was a series of biographies of Roman emperors from Augustus to Vitellius, now only extant in fragments primarily represented by *Galba* and *Otho*, two of the short-lived emperors of 69 CE. Imperial biography was *en vogue* among the Greco-Roman elite, who were still coming to terms with life under autocratic rule: Plutarch's Roman contemporary Suetonius composed his famous *Lives of the Caesars* during roughly the same period. Plutarch's greatest contribution to the genre of biography was the *Parallel Lives*, a work that has inspired biographers from Late Antiquity, the Renaissance, the Enlightenment and American Revolution, up to the present day. This lengthy work, composed during the final two decades of Plutarch's life, consists of paired biographies of Greek and Roman statesmen (24 pairs in total, with 23 extant). In the *Parallel Lives*, all of Plutarch's precedents are dead and had been for quite some time. His Roman subjects range from Romulus and the foundation of Rome in the 8th century BCE to Mark Antony and the fall of the Republic in 31 BCE. The Greek subjects reach into the mythological past with the legendary Athenian founder Theseus and end with the Achaean general Philopoemen (253–183 BCE), the "last of the Greeks" before Rome conquered Greece herself.

Plutarch dedicated the series to Sosius Senecio, a prominent Roman who had twice been designated consul (99 and 107 CE), the highest executive office attainable to those outside the line of succession, and was connected to Pliny the Younger and the emperor Trajan. Senecio exemplifies the readership Plutarch had in mind as he wrote: prominent politically active men of the Greek *and* Roman elite who were intellectually engaged and committed to their own lifelong development through engagement with philosophy, history, literature, and the arts. These readers, men of action and education, were expected not merely to absorb the biographical narratives but also to analyze and evaluate the characters contained within, and to adapt their examples of judgment, moral behavior, and leadership to their own particular context. Susan Jacobs has recently described the narratives Plutarch composed for such readers as "pragmatic biography", which uses narratives of political lives to examine two main questions:

> First, how do particular qualities of character contribute to, or impede, the ability of a statesman to achieve beneficial outcomes for his city? Secondly, how do they interact with the other factors at work—namely, a man's practical judgment, persuasiveness, and good or bad fortune—to strengthen or undermine his achievements as a leader?[1]

Thus, while the content of the *Parallel Lives* was historical, their primary function was practical pedagogy, aimed at a readership with enough direct experience of political life to be able to critically assess the decisions and characters of the protagonists.

Plutarch composed each pair as a stand-alone book with a brief introduction to the pairing and a formal *synkrisis*, or comparison, as a capstone, although we do find some variation in that formula.[2] The prefaces tend to highlight Plutarch's rationale behind the pairing, commonly citing similarities of character or historical circumstance between the two men, while occasionally mentioning how a given pair fits within the larger context of the collection as a whole. Plutarch also used the prefaces to express his own view of or relationship to his writing. In general, the Greek *Life* is followed by its Roman counterpart, although the *Publicola-Solon*, *Fabius Maximus-Pericles*, and *Sertorius-Eumenes* pairs are exceptions. No matter whether the Greek or Roman comes first, Plutarch tends to use the first biography to introduce key issues of virtue and leadership, whereas the second biography complicates those ideas.[3] The narratives encompass the entire lives of the subjects as Plutarch's sources allowed him but are not limited to a "cradle to grave" scope: discussion of family lineage often precedes the birth of the protagonist, and his death may be followed by an epilogue on the outcomes of his descendants or, as in the case of Cleopatra in the *Antony*, Plutarch may choose to follow the lives of other key players to their conclusion, too.[4] Plutarch is selective in his choice of content for his biographies, exaggerating or downplaying different aspects of his protagonists' lives in order to bring to the fore the key questions he wants readers to focus on in that particular pair.[5] Indeed, he is explicit that his aim is not the determination and exposition of absolute historical fact, but rather the representation of the moral character (*Alex.* 1.1)[6]:

> For it is not Histories that I am writing, but Lives; and in the most illustrious deeds this is not always a manifestation of virtue or vice, nay, a slight thing like a phrase or a jest often makes a greater revelation of character than battles where thousands fall.

Thus, Plutarch's narratives rely heavily on historical anecdotes, memorable quotations, imagined dialogues, and editorializing remarks on the subject by characters internal to the narrative as well as the narrator himself. Plutarch uses the final formal comparison to distinguish between the subjects on criteria of virtue, judgment, or fortune. Competition, or the question of who is the better man, is implicit in these comparisons, but Plutarch rarely makes a firm decision in the favor of one or the other with regards to all criteria.

It is a common misconception that Plutarch's biographical subjects are all "heroes", models of virtues worthy of imitation in all aspects. In the past four decades, however, Plutarch scholars have agreed that his moralism does not consist of simple prescriptions (i.e., "do X", "don't do Y"), but rather is "descriptive" and "exploratory", often including multiple contrasting perspectives as he conducts an examination of the virtue and vices, successes and failures, of his subjects.[7] While Plutarch wished to improve himself and his readers through the *Lives* so that they could become better men and more effective leaders, he neither expected nor fabricated moral perfection in any of his subjects. His chosen protagonists are generally admirable but not all of them; at the same time, even the worst among them are shown to have some admirable qualities. Plutarch explicitly states that the Hellenistic king Demetrius and the Roman general Mark Antony are negative exempla, but—perhaps relevant for the present volume—they are nevertheless instrumental to the continuing education of public leaders precisely *because* they hone the reader's ability to determine what is worthy of imitation. Not only do such cautionary tales teach us how not to act, our knowledge of them spurs us on to do better: "we also shall be more eager to observe and imitate the better lives if we are not left without narratives of the blameworthy and the bad" (*Demetr.* 1.6).

Plutarch could, and did, write moralizing political biographies as singletons and in a series, so it is a fair question to ask what the advantages of the approach of parallel biography were over writing about his subjects individually.[8] If we abstract Plutarch's driving question as "How do moral character, effective leadership, and historical context affect one another?", we can see how writing in paired lives enabled Plutarch to break this grand inquiry into manageable conceptual chunks, to foster nuanced moral perspectives and active reader engagement. Let us first consider how parallel biographies sharpened Plutarch's ability to focus his reader's attention on a few select aspects of his subjects' characters.

The whole book works together to this effect. The preface primes the reader to attend to certain points of similarity. The exaggeration or diminution of details to highlight the connections between lives and the revisiting of similar scenarios and traits across the two *Lives* allows Plutarch to use repetition and variation to emphasize the issues he saw as significant and worthy of reflection in a given pair. The reading of the second *Life* reinforces the moral and leadership issues raised by the first, and finally the comparison (when it is present) reminds the reader one last time of issues they ought to have paid attention to, or perhaps should revisit. Moreover, the paired structure allows Plutarch to complicate the reader's ideas of human character and political leadership by examining similar scenarios with certain variables (individual, organization, or external) changed and then observing the outcomes. Through these variations on a theme, Plutarch's reader is encouraged to explain and understand for themselves why individuals with similar traits or who made similar decisions had different outcomes, or how very different approaches may have led to similar results.

Paired biography by its very nature invites the reader to actively engage in finding points of comparison and contrast between the protagonists; in other words, readers seek to make sense of why these two individuals are "in the same conversation". Plutarch's style of writing, with its frequent use of internal and editorial evaluations of his subjects, further elicits the reader's engagement by adding in a strong element of moral evaluation.[9] In the formal comparisons, for example, Plutarch models how one way in which the reader could apply his own capacity for moral deliberation to the men at hand, while also inviting the reader's active engagement in weighing whether or not he agrees with Plutarch's assessment. Utilizing these narrative techniques of reader engagement, parallel biography invites the reader to extract seemingly timeless lessons from the past that could be applied to the present reader's own life. Plutarch's grand series of paired lives offers an abundance of "data points" of lived experience, rich with the cultural, historical, political, and psychological "metadata" that he weaves into the narrative. This collection of qualitative data on human life encourages the reader to see patterns within human character, social behavior, and political leadership that appear consistent across time and culture and, therefore, have potential relevance to one's own circumstances. In the preface to the *Timoleon-Aemilius Paullus* pair, Plutarch shares a glimpse into his own engagement with his writing subjects and the impact it has had on his life (*Tim.* 1.1–3):

> I began the writing of my "Lives" for the sake of others, but I find that I am continuing the work and delighting in it now for my own sake also, using history as a mirror and endeavoring in a manner to fashion and adorn my life in conformity with the virtues therein depicted. For the result is like nothing else than daily living and associating together, when

> I receive and welcome each subject of my history in turn as my guest, so to speak, and observe carefully "how large he was and of what mien," and select from his career what is most important and most beautiful to know . . . But in my own case, the study of history and the familiarity with it which my writing produces, enables me, since I always cherish in my soul the records of the noblest and most estimable characters, to repel and put far from me whatever base, malicious, or ignoble suggestion my enforced associations may intrude upon me, calmly and dispassionately turning my thoughts away from them to the fairest of my examples.

Plutarch's expectation would be that his readers would follow his example in their engagement and integration of the lessons of his *Parallel Lives* into their own lives.[10] In sum, parallel biography enabled Plutarch to focalize and complicate his explorations of human political life and to actively engage his readers and invite them to make their own meaning from history.

Before moving on to survey American biographical works with an explicit Plutarchan framing, it would be remiss of me to overlook a key aspect of the *Parallel Lives*: the undercurrent of grand Greco-Roman cultural comparison. Although it is less salient to this *Dead Precedents* volume, other authors of American biography have found it to be central to their own Plutarchan inspiration. Undoubtedly, Plutarch's choice to consistently pair Greeks with Romans over a series of twenty-four books begs the question of what Plutarch was saying about the two dominant cultures of his world. However, what Plutarch's ultimate aim was in squaring up Greeks and Romans remains a matter of debate among Plutarch scholars. Was he trying to prove the military prowess of the Greeks to their Roman rulers, or to demonstrate the Hellenic virtue of the Roman conquerors to his fellow Greeks? Was he voicing resistance or resignation to the current state of affairs? Or were the *Parallel Lives* an attempt to create a common treasury of exempla for the increasingly interconnected, bicultural Greco-Roman elite of the 2nd century CE?[11] It would be unfair and inaccurate to pigeonhole Plutarch into one consistent viewpoint: throughout the *Parallel Lives*, one can sense both pride and nostalgia, admiration and disdain as reactions to both the Greek and Roman past. For our purposes, it may suffice to say that Plutarch viewed all of Greco-Roman history as rich with teachable moments for his contemporary readers—Greek and Roman alike—to apply towards their personal lives and public careers.

Now that we are better acquainted with our muse from Chaeronea, let us examine how "Plutarch" has been abstracted into a symbol of biographical writing in America. Plutarch's influence on the ideas of the Founding Fathers, especially Alexander Hamilton, has been studied thoroughly, as has his reception by Ralph Waldo Emerson and other thinkers of the American Enlightenment.[12] Rather than revisiting that well-worn territory, I will instead focus on four lesser-known texts that proclaim their Plutarchan inspiration in their titles: *The*

Columbian Plutarch (1819), *The American Plutarch* (1964), *An Anglo-American Plutarch* (1990), and *A Modern Plutarch* (2016). The goal of this survey will be to explore the range of ways that American historical biographers have departed from or remained faithful to the Plutarchan source and thereby be able to more clearly delineate the contours of the present volume's own inspiration.

The Columbian Plutarch; or an exemplification of several distinguished American Characters, written by Thomas Woodward and printed in Philadelphia in 1819, states that "the object of this publication is to extend some information respecting several of the most eminent and distinguished men in North America, from its first discovery to the present time" (v).[13] The twenty-eight narratives are arranged in chronological order from Christopher Columbus to Thomas Jefferson. There is no attempt to pair lives, but the introduction clearly indicates that the unspoken comparison for America's great men is the entire world: "The people of the land of Washington, Franklin, Rittenhouse, Rush, and Hamilton, may dispute the palm of philosophy, and patriotism, with any other nation of the globe" (v). Woodward praises Plutarch's biographies for both their charming writing and their valuable content, citing an anonymous "late writer" for the view that biography at its best "encourages the timid, gives hope to the desponding, rouses the inactive, furnishes the enterprising with a chart for their conduct, and teaches everyone to turn to the best account, the powers and means with which he is entrusted" (iv). Evidently, Plutarch represented to Woodward the gold standard of morally edifying, pragmatic biography. He viewed parallelism as ornamental, rather than fundamental to Plutarch's writing. By composing a "Plutarch" for the young American nation, Woodward moreover asserts its standing in the history of "great civilizations" and positions its men of action as worthy objects of admiration.

The American Plutarch: 18 Lives Selected from the Dictionary of American Biography (1964) re-centers parallelism as the key feature of Plutarchan biography but in a highly superficial way.[14] The goal of the collection was to make a medley of the *Dictionary of American Biography* that would be appealing for a popular audience, and it seems likely that branding this volume with the recognized name "Plutarch" was intended to increase its literary caché. Howard Mumford Jones in his introduction to the volume writes that "Plutarch has meant a great deal to thoughtful Americans" (xvi). He acknowledges that earlier American readers of Plutarch treated his *Lives* as pragmatic biography: "One has to but read John Adams or Thomas Jefferson to discover how these examples from antiquity sank in and how Plutarch was read as a series of practical lessons in the management of states" (xviii). The biographies were selected and paired by the editor, Edward T. James, from a pre-existing collection written by multiple biographers, *The Dictionary of American Biography* (first published in 1928). The original authors only made minor revisions for the 1964 collection, "rework[ing] wherever necessary in light of new evidence" (xvi). James himself did not write any of the biographies, nor did he add any formal comparisons, leaving all such analytical work to the reader. The introduction further reveals a tone of benevolent disdain for Plutarch's penchant for anecdote and quotation. Jones emphasized that the biographies chosen for this collection were vetted by the rigorous editing process of *The Dictionary of American Biography*, producing the "utmost accuracy", whereby "the governing principle in this collection is demonstrable truth" (xix). The historical value of biography is elevated above the moral, and the modern objective biographer is set against the conversational ancient model. Moreover, unlike *The Columbian Plutarch*, which implicitly measured Americans against figures from more established cultures, *The American Plutarch* measures American against American. The pairs were arranged loosely on a North–South dichotomy, but Jones also lists "genuine differences of value and of approach to creating a nation" as another vector along which subjects are compared and contrasted. Thus, *The American Plutarch* merely invokes "Plutarch" to indicate a literary pedigree and provide a basic framework for repackaging a dry reference text into a form more engaging to a certain kind of educated reader.

An Anglo-American Plutarch (1990) maintains both its source's pairing of biographies and its pairing of civilizations.[15] Formally, it is far more like the *Parallel Lives* than the aforementioned volumes. For the most part, it is the work of a single author, David Burton.[16] Benjamin Franklin stands as a singleton, followed by ten pairs, each of which is capped by a *synkrisis*-like "Comment". Burton is willing to engage with the moral benefits of pragmatic biography, invoking former British Prime Minister Herbert Asquith's view that biography "brings comfort, enlarges sympathy, expels selfishness, quickens aspiration", much in the same vein as Woodward's approach to the genre. Burton draws on a perceived (and highly simplistic) similarity between the relationship Greece and Rome had with each other to that of England and America. The primary goal of the collection is to illustrate the nuances of that relationship (vii):

> The cast of characters as it has been finally assembled does, nonetheless, tell much about the two civilizations which have sources in a common culture, as well as the nurturing relationship between an erstwhile mother country and its vigorous scion.

In his epilogue to the volume, Burton highlights how the value of the collection is greater than the sum of its parts (287):

> It is not in the individual or paired lives that the moral dimension of the Angelo-Americans is most persuasive, however, but in the collective biography of so varied a number. Taken all in all, these personal accounts do not pretend to a moral superiority for the individuals, much less for the nations involved. What is worthy of note is that rarely have two great peoples exhibited so many of the same fundamental principles in the course of their separate developing histories.

Burton is thus relatively faithful to the form of the *Parallel Lives*, and similarly seeks to create a common biographical source from which people of two distinct, but closely interrelated cultures can draw inspiration.

Most recently, *A Modern Plutarch: Comparisons of the Most Influential Modern Statesmen* (2016) by Robert Lloyd George resumes the theme of Anglo-American comparison but with a distinctive perspective.[17] George, a Welshman and descendant of the World War I British Prime Minister of the same name, made his career in the United States. As he learned more about American history, he felt himself to be an "Old World historian" in the New World and imagining that Plutarch must have had a similar feeling as he tried to make sense of the Romans. The volume's stated goal is to educate George's British compatriots on American figures who may be less well known to them. In his twenty-five brief pairs, George does not strive to rewrite history or do original research, happily includes quotations and anecdotes, and includes a formal *synkrisis* with each pair. He uses a variety of different similarities to determine his pairs, whether it is a shared profession, "like paths", or historical circumstances. In his preface, he does nod towards the reader's active engagement in evaluating his choice of subjects: "everyone will have a different view as to who are the most significant figures and with whom they might be compared" (xiii). The only one of the surveyed biographers who ever met with or interviewed any of his subjects (and only two, at that), George recognizes the merits of turning to dead precedents: "it is too soon to write about living statesmen; the verdict of history must wait until some time after their passing" (5). Of the four volumes surveyed, *The Modern Plutarch* alone maintains the form, style, and pragmatic approach of the *Parallel Lives* while also adopting Plutarch as a personal role model for the author.

So, how does *Dead Precedents* fit into this tradition of American biography inspired by Plutarch? The idea of cultural competition seen in Burton and George, and implied in Woodward, is absent from the present volume. The chapters herein are unpaired, although not unparalleled: behind every contribution looms an unwritten narrative of the Trump presidency, silently constructed from the experiences and memories of each author and reader alike. Plutarch himself was not unfamiliar with invoking but not providing a parallel narrative. In his *Virtues of Women*, a collection of historical anecdotes about the heroic undertakings of women aimed at proving that "the virtue of a man and of a woman are one and the same", Plutarch mentions the names of several great men with whom similarly great women could be compared. He even seems to promise that he will include men's narratives to complement those of his heroines, but the extant text does not fulfill that expectation.[18] In Plutarch's case, it may be that his readers could easily conjure up the obvious *comparandi* for themselves, or could even pluck them directly from the *Parallel Lives*. In *Dead Precedents*, each contributor forges their own links between their material and Trump, and each reader will likely have the period so fresh in mind that it would be tedious to rehearse the details. Or perhaps Trump's presidency is simply too recent (perhaps even too traumatic) for one to construct a coherent and comprehensive narrative, especially given the fact that Trump continues to wield significant political influence and even is considering a future presidential campaign. However it may be, the "silent parallel" is yet another technique by which biographical parallelism can spark active reader engagement, encouraging us to measure the historical narratives of this volume against our own experience of recent events.

On a related note, this volume uses the implied parallel, as well as the series format, to make an examination of the nature, meaning, and impact of Trump's presidency both more manageable to comprehend and more complex. Each contributor's perspective and specialized expertise enables them to highlight a different aspect of Trump's presidency through comparison with the past, and the connections that transcend contributions add nuance to our understanding of issues such as demagoguery, image-cultivation, and tyranny. The range of historical and cultural perspectives on these issues represented here invites the reader, as Plutarch does, to extract timeless lessons about leadership and the challenges of democracy and, ideally, to apply them to the present and future. For while there is, as Burton and Woodward both allude to, a certain comfort deriving from knowing that others before us have survived through similar times of crisis, there is simultaneously an anxiety that comparative historical inquiries may elicit. If such events or individuals occurred both before and now, what will stop them from happening in the future? If history repeats itself, will we be better equipped to anticipate it, respond to it, or perhaps even avoid or resist it? Ultimately, the Plutarchan inspiration for *Dead Precedents* may not manifest itself so much in formal characteristics but instead in the impulse to turn to pragmatic, comparative biography to make meaning of historical events and prepare us to live and lead better in the future.

Notes

1 Susan G. Jacobs, *Plutarch's Pragmatic Biographies* (Leiden: Brill, 2018), 417.

2 Of the twenty-three extant pairs, eleven pairs follow the preface-two Lives-*synkrisis* model, while two pairs lack a *synkrisis*, seven others lack a formal prologue, and two pairs have neither.

3 Tim Duff, *Plutarch's Lives: Exploring Virtue and Vice* (Oxford: Oxford University Press, 1999).

4 Christopher Pelling, *Plutarch and History* (Swansea: Classical Press of Wales, 1997), 365–386.

5 B. Bosworth, "History and Artifice in Plutarch's *Eumenes*," in Philip A. Stadter (ed.), *Plutarch and the Historical Tradition* (London: Routledge, 1992), 56–89 provides a case-study of Plutarch's manipulation of historical material to reinforce the themes of the pair in the *Sertorius-Eumenes*.

6 All translations of Plutarch's *Lives* are from Perrin's translations for the Loeb Classical Library series (Cambridge, MA: Harvard University Press, 1918–1919).

7 See Pelling, *Plutarch and History*, 349–364 and Duff, *Plutarch's Lives*, 243–309 for further discussion of *synkrisis*.

8 *Aratus* and *Artaxerxes* are two other extant Plutarchan biographies that do not fall within the projects of the *Lives of the Caesars* or the *Parallel Lives*. They nevertheless share the same approach to biographical writing and moralizing didactic aims of Plutarch's other works.

9 Chrysanthos S. Chrysanthou, *Plutarch's Parallel Lives—Narrative Technique and Moral Judgement* (Berlin: de Gruyter, 2018).

10 Tim Duff, "Plutarch's *Lives* and the Critical Reader," in G. Roskam and L. van der Stockt (eds.), *Virtues for the People: Aspects of Plutarchan Ethics* (Leuven: Leuven University Press, 2011), 59–82.

11 For these various views on Plutarch's attitude towards Rome, see C. P. Jones, *Plutarch and Rome* (Oxford: Clarendon Press, 1971); Simon Swain, *Hellenism and Empire: Language, Classicism and Power in the Greek World* (Oxford: Clarendon Press, 1996); Tim Whitmarsh, *Greek Literature and the Roman Empire: The Politics of Imitation* (Oxford: Oxford University Press, 2001); Christopher Pelling, "Plutarch's 'Tale of Two Cities': Do the *Parallel Lives* Combine as Global Histories?" in Noreen Humble (ed.), *Plutarch's Lives: Parallelism and Purpose* (Swansea: Classical Press of Wales, 2010), 217–236.

12 On Plutarch and Emerson, see Ronald Bosco, "'What Poems Are Many Private Lives': Emerson Writing the American Plutarch," *Studies in the Literary Imagination*, vol. 27, no. 1 (1994), 103–129. On Plutarch and the Founding Fathers, see P. Stadter, "Alexander Hamilton's Notes on Plutarch in His Paybook," in P. Stadter (ed.), *Plutarch and His Roman Readers* (Oxford: Oxford University Press, 2011), 214–330 and Carl J. Richard, "Plutarch and the Early American Republic," in Mark Beck (ed.), *A Companion to Plutarch* (Chichester; Malden, MA: Wiley Blackwell, 2014), 598–610.

13 Thomas Woodward, *The Columbian Plutarch; or an Exemplification of Several Distinguished American Characters* (Philadelphia, 1819).

14 Edward T. James, ed., *The American Plutarch: 18 Lives Selected from the Dictionary of American Biography* (New York: Scribner, 1964).

15 David Henry Burton et al., *An Anglo-American Plutarch* (Lanham, MD: University Press of American, 1990).

16 Esmond Wright, Phillip T. Smith, and Antoinette M. Burton wrote four of the twenty-one biographies.

17 Robert Lloyd George, *A Modern Plutarch: Comparisons of the Most Influential Modern Statesmen* (New York: Abrams, 2016).

18 Monaco Caterine, "Tyrannical Men and Virtuous Women in Plutarch's *Mulierum Virtutes*," *Illinois Classical Studies*, vol. 44, no. 1 (2019), 194–208 provides an overview of this text with a particular emphasis on how Plutarch uses contrasts between his heroines and tyrants to substantiate his thesis of moral gender equality.

3

THE POLITICS OF ANGER

Donald Trump and Cleon of Athens

Mark A. Menaldo

American politics are in a bad way.[1] Unrestrained voices, rejection of norms, and opposition carry the day. In the last four years, many lamented that the country had descended into tribal warfare.[2] Waving one's partisan battle flag seems like the new patriotism. As I write this chapter, many months after the 2020 presidential election, Trump's 2020 flags are still flying in my county and I have recently sighted a 2024 "Save America Again." Why did politics lapse into such rage these last four years, with partisans of opposing sides feeling all-time highs of frustration, fear, and anger with each other?[3]

The Donald Trump presidency made it okay to unfurl one's political anger in a persistent and voluble way. As early as 2016, during the primaries, Trump said: "As far as I am concerned, anger is okay. Anger and energy is what this country needs."[4] For his followers, Trump's anger is cathartic, and, I would argue, it makes him seem strong and competent, especially in comparison to his rivals. Aware of this effect, early in his primary run, Trump pegged Jeb Bush as "low energy," the wonkish bespectacled former Governor of Florida. His derisive nickname for Hillary Clinton was "crooked Hillary," and, in the 2020 election, he nicknamed Joe Biden, "sleepy Joe."

His presidency was combustible, and his "stop the steal" post-election rallying cry and incitement of the January 6 Capitol riots almost set the country ablaze. With Donald Trump's electoral defeat, many want to turn the page on the last four years and stop feeding this narcissist's ego. I include myself in this group. Despite our collective Trump fatigue and hopes that his presidency was a momentary blip for American democracy, I believe it is misguided to think that cool reason and calm tempers will prevail in the future. The seething political madness that gripped the country under Trump is not over, notwithstanding Joe Biden's overwhelming victory—Biden received not only a majority of the popular vote

DOI: 10.4324/9781003110361-3

but also the largest vote percentage against an incumbent president since 1932. Despite Biden's promises of bipartisanship, little remains of the moderate middle and ideological overlap between the main parties.[5] Moreover, Trump's preternatural ability to stir all kinds of angry emotions revealed an unruly and barbaric strain in American culture.[6] Politics as usual, we now can see, was the retardant to America's latent anger and resentment. Trump was its accelerant.

With the blueprint laid out for the next Trump-like politician, it is duly vital for us to look back on Trump's "winning" strategy of picking fights and understand how he made anger his followers' drug of choice. In a broader sense, the peculiar character of Trump's presidency reveals how the underlying emotions of anger in a democratic people can lead to disorders that wear down the republican institutions that the founders supplied as a bulwark against the turmoil and convulsions of democracy.

Specifically, I argue that throughout his candidacy and presidency, culminating in the January 6 riot at the US Capitol, Donald Trump was the most violent man in America and this quality of his rhetoric made him incredibly persuasive among his supporters. People familiar with Thucydides' *History of the Peloponnesian War* will recognize that I am cutting an idea from this ancient tome and grafting it to American politics. In Book III of his *History*, the classical Athenian writer describes Cleon "as the most violent citizen and much the most persuasive speaker with the demos at that time" (3.36.6). I contend that by examining these two political figures side by side, and understanding them, we can avoid Trump-like men in the future. We can understand them better because they belong to the same political genus.

Despite these men's close affinities, there is little in the way of comparison between the two.[7] Many commentators have compared Trump and his cult of personality to modern fascists and strongmen such as Hitler, Mussolini, Latin American caudillos, and African dictators.[8] But these comparisons fail to link Trump to his consummate skill, which was to become, like Cleon, the leader of the *demos* (the People).[9] Moreover, Trump succeeded in a country that people presumed to have overcome what James Madison observed as the inherent flaw of *pure* democracies, which is its tendency toward faction.[10] Scholars and concerned citizens alike must understand Trump's effect on American democracy by comparing him to political kin.

The ancient Greeks, as borne out in their literature, were steeped in emotions, such as pity, anger, fear, love, and jealousy, and "the first word of what is probably the earliest Greek poem to survive—the Iliad—is 'wrath.'"[11] From Homer's many terms for anger (*menis*, *cholos*, *nemesis*) to Plato's and Aristotle's hope to tame the volatile *thumos* (spiritedness), the range of meanings for anger, from Homer to Plato, is culturally specific and, simultaneously, universal.[12] The two masters of populism I discuss show how despite perfunctory political ideologies, invective-filled rhetoric easily creates widespread suspicion of elites and foreign dangers. Cleon's and Trump's angry politics flow from an ineluctable political necessity, which is to stoke the instinctual and visceral emotions of the demos: fear, anger, and resentment.[13]

Cleon

Cleon's biographical information comes down to us solely from his critics. However, these classical writers' powers of observation are so deft that by describing what was worst about Cleon, they also hint at the hidden appeal of his methods. It's just the same with Trump, I argue. What the critic might find repellent about Trump is what keeps his supporters in rapt attention and arouses their devotion and intense emotional responses.

Cleon was a "new politician" who was without noble ancestry, landed wealth, and, most importantly, military experience. Before Cleon, Athenian citizens viewed the *strategoi* (generals) as the only citizens fit for and worthy of political leadership. Cleon, through sheer political talent, managed to dominate the Athenian assembly and ushered in the rule of the *demagogoi* (demagogues).[14] What we know about Cleon that is available to us today comes from his foremost critics, Aristophanes, Thucydides, Aristotle, and Plutarch.

Aristophanes, like Thucydides, was Cleon's contemporary. Yet, unlike the sober and tragic Thucydides, Aristophanes was Athens's greatest comedian, and he always veiled Cleon in a fictional character whose qualities were that of a low-born vulgarian and a corrupt, venal politician. The comic mocked him for being a leather merchant (Archanians 299–300). In ancient Athens, sellers were looked down upon by aristocrats, and leather tanning, an incredibly filthy and foul-smelling enterprise, was universally despised. Moreover, in *Knights*, a play about Cleon, Aristophanes says that he "falsely slanders" and "takes bribes" (65–67). There is no evidence of Cleon ever taking bribes. Still, Aristophanes' disdain for the Peloponnesian war—which he squarely blamed Pericles for—and Cleon's zealous hawkishness may have motivated the poet to try and make the mud stick. Nevertheless, this unconventional political man succeeded, despite Aristophanes's best efforts.

A century later, Aristotle casts Cleon in a nasty political light but is silent about the pecuniary gains Aristophanes accuses him of. He says,

> and the leader of the people was Cleon, son of Cleaenetus, who seemed to have corrupted the people more than anyone by his attacks; he was the first to shout while speaking in the assembly, first to use abusive language there, first to hitch up his skirts [and move about] while addressing the people, although the other speakers behaved properly.
>
> *(Constitution of Athens 28.3)*

In Aristotle's critical verdict of Cleon, it is here that we first see the negative connotation of the word demagogue. Writing centuries later, and echoing Aristotle's judgment, Plutarch says that Cleon came to:

> increase his reputation and power so much that he entered upon a phase of insolent pride and ungovernable boldness, during which he inflicted

> upon the city various disasters, not the least of which was that he stripped the rostrum of its decorum.
>
> *(Lives, Nicias, 8)*

Cleon would certainly not pass "presidential" muster in American politics, as many commentators have observed about his contemporary analogue, "The Donald."[15]

Thucydides reports to the reader that Cleon ascends to power in Athens in 429 BCE. His leadership over the demos contrasts sharply with Pericles, the Athenian statesman who presided over Athens's "Golden Age."[16] While in power, Pericles steered Athens's imperial power prudently and engineered a building program that made Athens the "school of Hellas." As a direct democracy with no executive branch, Athenian political life depended upon persuasive speech in the assembly. Pericles was Athens's greatest speaker, and he combined an elevation of purpose and dignity of language. Plutarch's and Thucydides' account of Pericles provides an image of an enlightened rationalist known for his Olympian loftiness and composure, a political actor who could derive authority through self-command and persuasive speech. Like Athens, America witnessed Barack Obama's meteoric rise, legalistic mind, and measured tone. Obama combined big ambitions to change American society through social policy with an instinctive moderation that accommodated various camps, interests, and agendas.

In his most famous speech, recounted by Thucydides, known to us as "The Funeral Oration," Pericles makes Athens's democracy glow to inspire its citizens to live up to its ideals. However, in the second year of the war, which turned out to be a 27 year affair, Athens suffered a significant blow to her efforts. A plague that began in sub-Saharan Africa made its way to Athens. By some estimates, it killed upward of a third of the population, which numbered 250,000–300,000.[17] Pericles also died from the plague, and, after him, there was no political leader to which Athens could turn. After his death, Thucydides tells us that Pericles' prudent leadership was lost amid policies that allowed "private ambitions and private interests, in matters apparently quite foreign to the war, to lead them into projects unjust both to themselves and to their allies" (2.65).

The Mytilene Debate: Kill Them All

Cleon comes on the scene in the fourth year of the war and we bear witness to his hawkish response to Mytilene, a free ally of Athens, which tries to revolt from Athens's Imperial league. To make matters worse, Mytilene had consorted with Sparta, Athens's mortal enemy. The Athenians put down the rebellion and captured the Mytilene oligarchs (about 1000) and a Spartan named Salaithos, responsible for the revolt, and sent them to Athens (3.35 ff.). The Athenians immediately put Salaithos to death, despite his promise to help withdraw the Peloponnesians from a strategic allied city of Platea. Enraged at the Spartan interference in their imperial affairs, the hasty Athenians ignore their foreign policy interests. Had they unburned themselves of the Spartan siege at Platea, the war would have decidedly tilted in their favor. Thucydides tells us that in anger (*orgē*) they "voted to put to death not only the men there but also all Mytilenean adult males and to enslave the children and women." The reasons they give for this punishment are a general condemnation of the revolt and the added insult that Mytilene abused their privileged position (3.36). Mytilene and only two other allies "had never been reduced to subjection and tribute but had retained her walls and her fleet, continuing long prosperous and free."[18]

The very next day, Thucydides tells us, the Athenians regretted their cruel and savage decision to execute all the citizens as opposed to only the guilty. The Athenians then took the unusual step of taking up deliberation once again, yet this did not prove difficult since "a majority of citizens wanted someone to make it possible for them to deliberate again" (3.36). However, there is a crucial difficulty facing the Athenians; they are pressed for time as they duly dispatched a fleet at once to enforce the resolution the day before. Thucydides presents Cleon's speech first in the ensuing debate and an opposing speech by Diodotus follows him.

Thucydides, as stated earlier, describes Cleon as the most violent man in Athens and the most persuasive among the *demos*, and his speech demonstrates the influence of his violent rhetoric. Although Diodotus' motion carries the day, which is that the Athenians attenuate their prior decree and not massacre all the Mytilenians (men), Cleon's speech is both his rhetorical debut and the first speaker the reader hears from since Pericles in the *History*.[19]

Thucydides' intention with recreating this debate points the reader to learning not only the character of the new Athenian leadership but also the latent weaknesses of the democracy, which is its vulnerability to certain violent and emotional politics, driven by resentment. Pericles' extraordinary leadership created a bulwark against the demos' vacillating of emotional reactions. Pericles could steer the demos to his rational policies by, as Plutarch says, "making that use of hopes and fears, as his two chief rudders."[20] Cleon, I shall explain, disdains prudence and enjoins the Athenians to return to the feelings of anger that led to the original resolution that won the day. It becomes evident by his speech that this was his resolution. To do so, Cleon sows distrust against things foreign, the enemy abroad and the enemy within, that is, the reasoned speech of Athenian elites.[21]

Cleon's speech is "rambling, contradictory, and vehement," yet what it lacks in philosophical insight is more than made up for by dint of its being a masterpiece of populism.[22] Cleon presents himself as a man of the people instead of the brainy and grandiloquent speakers who he warns will try to change the Athenians' hearts and minds. Simultaneously, Cleon stands apart from the demos; he is shrewder than they and, therefore, knows their true interests better than they do. Like Donald Trump, he advised the Athenians by "telling them like it is." He warns his fellow Athenians that they live in critical danger of undermining the city's stability because they forget that their empire is a tyranny.[23] The empire provides them with domestic tranquility. Athens's superior power and not its goodwill make its allies toe the line (3.37).

Yet, there is an even greater danger, thinks Cleon, which is that democracy falters and cannot stay on course in policy matters. He believes that the virtue of a political community is its ability to stick to the laws it proposes without deviation, no matter how insensible those laws might be. He argues that ignorance combined with self-control is a virtue, while cleverness is a vice. Cleon is singling out the smooth talkers who seek repute from dazzling displays of rhetoric in the assembly. These political sophisticates are vain and self-aggrandizing. For Cleon, these men are not interested in the commonweal but have a selfish agenda: to prevail over their competitors in public displays of eloquence. Cleon proceeds to remonstrate the demos while also sowing doubts about the allegiance of these fine speakers—Athens's "deep state" like resistors. Rather than allow the novelty of fine speeches delude them, Cleon thinks that the Athenians should turn their attention to those who re-opened up the debate about the Mytileaneans. What motivates them by coming to the aid of the guilty, especially now, as the embers of Athenian anger are going out? Cleon seeks to rekindle these by reminding the Athenians of reality; the Mytileaneans have harmed them in the worst way—by daring to act like the Athenians who pursue power for the sake of self-interest and not justice.

Cleon, either unaware or not entirely worried about his glaring contradiction, blames the privileged ally for not keeping their word by setting might above right and acting with insolence. The Mytileaneans are guilty of injustice, yet the Athenians are also at fault for granting the city a unique standing among the allies. Cleon's illogic leads to the following conclusion: as a tyranny, Athens can be the only city to set might above right, and in doing so it "rightfully" keeps the allies in equal subjection.

For Cleon, there is also the issue of deterrence. If they relent and only punish the main conspirators, Athens runs the risk of signaling a lack of resolve. And, he speculates, any ally will find the slightest pretext to revolt, knowing that the Athenians spared most of the Mytileaneans. Cleon wants the Athenians to remain steadfast in their resolved anger and forget the compassion that has contaminated their judgment. It is as if he were asking the Athenians, "Do you want to be imperialists or not?" Cleon claims that compassion does not befit an empire, and it is a feeling that only citizens can share with each other. Cleon's foreign policy puts Athens first.

Cleon ends his speech by urging the Athenians to regain their previous day's resolve by voting to uphold the original penalty for the crime. With their emotions blunted by remorse, their pleasure for words, and their failure to see the real danger they are in, the Athenians must find a way to return to their original feelings. Cleon's incendiary rhetoric is their conduit back to their anger, and angry punishment satisfies both the requirements of justice and advancing the city's interests.

Donald Trump

As a presidential candidate with no prior political experience, Trump ran as an outsider to the mainstream Washington establishment. Trump's famous slogan "drain the swamp" was a compelling metaphor that he used to communicate his ceaseless refrain, "the system is rigged." Trump was especially good at tapping into underlying conspiratorial notions felt by the American electorate, which existed well before launching his political career.[24]

But, on paper, Trump was the quintessential insider, a privileged one percenter since birth. Yet, his family did not secure a foothold in the upper echelons of New York society. Like Cleon, Trump was "new money," a boaster who claimed to possess vast sums of money, exceeding any need whatsoever. His residences' gilded glamour, flamboyant style, orange tan lines, comb-over hair, preference for fast food, and well-done steaks distanced him from established political and cultural elites. Trump was a coarse and crude brawler. As a pugilist, he bloodied his opponents with his bellicose and self-aggrandizing personality. His indecency, bravado, and ill-connected ideas won him a legion of followers, beyond his core constituency of less educated whites.[25]

In 2016, Hillary Clinton calculated badly, and labeled these people "deplorables," probably expecting that they would not turn out in the numbers needed for him to win the election. She and the world were shocked to learn how popular he became. The establishment politicians and cultural elite never understood this appeal. For example, he never had to worry about having an "arugula moment" by seeming out of touch with downscale voters on the stump, as did Barack Obama.[26]

Much like his ancient Athenian counterpart, Trump was also an easy target for comedians who parodied and spoofed him to no end. Some felt no need to resort to anything more than repeat what he said. There may not be a modern Aristophanes, but many talented comics, impersonators, and artists lampooning angles held up a mirror to Trump.[27] But the comedians failed, like Aristophanes, they misjudged how the man's audacity outstripped their efforts. Despite being ruthlessly mocked for four years, this had no effect on Trump and his following.

Trump was also something of a jokester and never broke character. He was pure hyperbole, full of outlandish expressions, routinely went off script, and insulted other people to no end. Neither self-deprecating nor given to laughter, Trump's sense of humor (if one can call it that) was inscrutable. The mockery of comic's failed to land a punch because Trump never made any attempt at claiming that he stood for virtue, character, or consistency. Pretending to be a good guy was for effete politicians, Trump's unseemliness was his appeal. Others ignored his unseemliness and excused it, but it was evidence of a raging and destructive mind. Trump never evolved; his violence is coeval with his personality.

From Golden Escalator to the January 6 Insurrection: Trump's Angry Politics

On June 15, 2016, Donald and Melania Trump descended on a golden escalator in the Manhattan tower that bears his name. He made his way to a makeshift platform and delivered an angry rant that broke the norms of mainstream political decorum. This was his Cleon moment. He lamented and criticized Mexico, America's losses to Asian countries, the Islamic State (or ISIS) turning terrorism into a business, the state of the economy, and Obamacare.

This bit of political theater launched Trump's path to the presidency. He never toned down his rhetoric, and his personality followed suit. He angered quickly, raved, and humiliated others. From his belligerent reality television character to his mockery of political rivals, Trump never cared about fulfilling the expectations of presidential characteristics, such as an even-keeled temperament. A master of twisting meanings for his purposes, Trump described his temperament in the following way during his 2016 candidacy: I think I have the best temperament or certainly one of the best temperaments of anybody that's ever run for the office of president. Ever, because I have a winning temperament. I know how to win.[28]

The telltale clue Trump gave about his temperament is his opinion of him as a winner. As a capitalist, he strived for gain, and he hurt people and firms in the process. As a politician, he yearned for power and would use the same game plan in politics. As a man without compassion, warmth, and closed off to mature disagreement, his pining for power took an aggressive form.[29] Trump identified plenty of foreign enemies and incensed the unfounded fears of millions of Americans, both ordinary people and conservative intellectuals who were inclined to think that the barbarians (immigrants) were at the gate.[30] His was an angry nationalism.

At the root of Trump's nationalism was his claim that the United States of America was the most just and exceptional nation ever to exist on Earth.[31] At the same time, Trump also lamented the loss of America's standing and the dilution of Americanness by non-American peoples and ideas. Like Cleon, Trump's relied on contradictions. America is at once the most extraordinary country but is also the world's chump. Trump and his followers are both a proud and sullen lot. As such, Trump was able to occupy two poles during his candidacy and term: America's exceptionalism and its decay. His popularity synthesized these two poles with his campaign slogan Make America Great Again (MAGA).

Donald Trump's encouragement of violence began during his candidacy. His rallies were amuck with his calls for violence against protesters. He also modeled the violence that he encouraged by making a spectacle of ejecting protesters. Once he became president, his pugilistic style did not subside. In his tweets, he attacked the media, immigrants, Muslims, and Black Lives Matter (BLM) protesters while never condemning white supremacist groups that perpetrated violence.[32] In the Charlottesville alt-right rally, which left a woman dead, he said there were "some very fine people on both sides."[33]

After George Floyd's murder at the hand of a police officer in 2020, protests erupted across the country. In Minnesota, Trump threatened to intervene militarily and tweeted, "when the looting starts the shooting starts," which, at the time, Twitter labeled as violating its rule glorifying violence.[34] Trump also made calls to "liberate" Michigan, and when protesters besieged the Capitol in Lansing, some armed, he tweeted: "The Governor of Michigan should give a little, and put out the fire," Trump then wrote "These are very good people, but they are angry. They want their lives back again, safely! See them, talk to them, make a deal."[35]

Trump's speech to supporters on January 6 was the culmination of his incendiary rhetoric. With the election over for months and all his legal challenges thrown out by the courts save one, Trump made one thing clear to his supporters, which is that they would have to fight.

"I said something's wrong here . . . and we fight. We fight like hell. And if you don't fight like hell, you're not going to have a country anymore."[36]

The so-called "Save America" march served to inflame Trump's supporters' fear and anger over what he repeatedly called a fraudulent election. Trump also puts his Vice-President Mike Pence in a bind by falsely telling the crowd that he had Constitutional authority to decertify the results. The mob stormed the Capitol, scaling walls, shattering windows, roaming halls, pepper spraying, and battering police officers. The crowd also chanted, "hang Mike Pence," and even strung up a noose from a tree. Photographs surfaced of lawmakers being evacuating, sheltering, hiding, ducking, and wearing gas masks.[37]

During the siege, Trump was slow to react to the violence; he wouldn't condemn the rioters, leading one unnamed official to call him "a total monster."[38] According to aides, Trump raged about perceived acts of betrayal, insisted that he had won the election, and only grudgingly accepted that his presidency was over. He read a prepared statement that expressed that there would be an orderly transition, yet never did he accept defeat.

Conclusion: Our Tragicomedy

After Cleon died in battle (his generalship began as a joke), Hyberbolus succeeded him. This new demagogue gained prominence and was as much a target of the comedians as his predecessor. He was the last of the Athenians to be ostracized and murdered by oligarchs on the island of Samos. Thucydides embodies the nadir of the Athenian empire in the Melian dialogue, a late episode later in the war where the Athenians slay the pious Melians to the last man. There is no Diodotus (or speech) that comes to the rescue. The final Athenian leader with substantial heft was Alcibiades. He was rhetorically brilliant, politically ingenious, and naturally gifted. Alcibiades masterminded the incredible yet catastrophic,

Sicilian expedition. The Athenian empire and democracy ended in defeat, losing to Sparta in a naval battle. The Spartans tore down Athens's vaunted long wall, put down their democracy, and installed the infamous tyranny of the thirty.

The storming of the Capitol was a combination of something at once violent and absurdly comical. There were dangerous elements within the mob who came ready to (potentially) take hostages and kill members of Congress. At the same time, people dressed in clownish costumes, took selfies, and streamed lived videos as if they were capturing their Capitol tour. Amid the visual cacophony, one stood out, the shirtless horned man, with red and white face paint, who left a note to then-Vice President Mike Pence saying, "It's only a matter of time, justice is coming."[39] Does one take this man and his warning seriously or has Trump imperiled our sensitivity to this action? We do not know whether to laugh or cry. Does this note and our collective response, in some sense, disclose the nadir of American democracy?

One only wonders what Aristophanes would have thought about the ridiculous and severe character of American violence and danger. Would Aristophanes have made a dent in Trump with his pen? Who might help us understand and help a comic, a sober historian, a sojourner? A new Alexis de Tocqueville with Nietzshe's insight and verve might be needed today to help examine all the complexity on the surface of American homespun simplicity, while also unearthing the darkness lurking in the souls of its people. Such a person will not care to restore America to greatness but, like Thucydides, can document its decline and, by doing so, help its citizens come to terms with this country's reality and manage it accordingly.

Notes

1 I would like to thank Lucas Allen, Andrew Baker, Ray Keck, and Alfonso Vergarary for reading previous drafts of this chapter and providing invaluable suggestions and feedback.

2 See Chua, "The Constitution is Threatened by Tribalism"; and Sullivan, "America Wasn't Built for Humans."

3 Pew Research Center, "Partisanship and Political Animosity in 2016."

4 Duhigg, "The Real Roots of American Rage."

5 Harrison, "The Forgotten Center."

6 Menaldo, "American Barbarism."

7 One notable exception is Bernard Dobsky's excellent scholarly essay, "Democracy, Demagogues, and Political Wisdom," 75–92.

8 See, for example, Ben-Ghiat, *Strongmen: Mussolini to the Present*; Encarnación, "American Caudillo."

9 For the Athenians, "Demos [meant] 'People,' as in the People of Athens, the body of citizens collectively. So, a young man was enrolled in his 'demos' (deme), and thus became a member of the 'Demos' (the People). As a member of the Demos, this young man could participate in the Assembly of Citizens that was the central institution of the democracy." Blackwell, "The Development of Athenian Democracy."

10 See Madison, *Federalist* No. 10.
11 Konstan, "Affect and Emotion in Greek Literature."
12 See Braund and Most, *Ancient Anger: Perspectives from Homer to Galen*; Kalimtzis, *Taming Anger: The Hellenic Approach to the Limitations of Reason*.
13 My analysis of Cleon is indebted to Timothy W. Burns's superb essay, "Anger in Thucydides and Aristophanes."
14 Lane, "Origins of the Statesman," 186.
15 For a trenchant critique of Trump's leadership style and upending of the presidency, see Hennessey and Wittes, *Unmaking the Presidency*.
16 For comprehensive accounts of Athenian politics and society and Pericles's leadership, see Cusher, "Thucydides on Innovative Leadership and its Limits," 327–352; Kagan, *Pericles of Athens and the Birth of Democracy*; and Menaldo, *Leadership and Transformative Ambition in International Relations*, 127–171.
17 Horgan, "The Plague at Athens."
18 Orwin, "The Humanity of Thucydides," 143.
19 I limit my discussion of the Mytilenean debate to Cleon's speech and save some remarks about Diodotus' speech for the conclusion. For a full interpretation of the debate, see
20 Menaldo, *Leadership and Transformative Ambition in International Relations*, 144.
21 The following Cleon's speech begins.
22 Orwin, "The Humanity of Thucydides," 144.
23 Compare to Pericles' speech in 2.63, which only after Athens is beset by the calamity of the plague, is he willing to grant that the Athenians hold their empire "like a tyranny."
24 See Uscinski, *Conspiracy Theories and the People Who Believe Them*.
25 McGill, "Out of Every 10 Trump Supporters, Nine Are White."
26 Romano, "How Does Obama Woo 'Downscale Dems'?"
27 See, for example, Cavna, "The Comedy that Got Inside Trump's Head."
28 Rosenthal, "The Trump Files."
29 See Fallows, "Reporter's Notebook."
30 I am referring here to Michael Anton's notorious 2016 article in the Claremont Review of Books, "The Flight 93 Election." In addition, since 2000–2016, there has been a steady decline of immigration into the United States while the U.S. population ages at a faster rate than it can replenish itself. See Last, *What to Expect When No One's Expecting*.
31 See Trump, "Mount Rushmore Speech."
32 Cineas, "Donald Trump is the accelerant."
33 Cathey and Keneally, "A Look Back at Trump Comments."
34 Cathey and Keneally, "A Look Back at Trump Comments."
35 Cathey and Keneally, "A Look Back at Trump Comments."
36 AP News, "Transcript of Trump's Speech."
37 To read about the number of arrests made and criminal charges brought by the Department of Justice against the rioters see, "Six Months Since the January 6th Attack on the Capitol," www.justice.gov/usao-dc/six-months-january-6th-attack-capitol.
38 Rucker, Parker, and Dawsey, "After Inciting Mob Attack, Trump Retreats in Rage. Then, Grudgingly, He Admits His Loss."
39 Billeaud, "Man Who Wore Horns, Hat Apologizes for Storming Capitol."

Bibliography

Anton, Michael. "The Flight 93 Election." *Claremont Review of Books*, September 5, 2016. https://claremontreviewofbooks.com/digital/the-flight-93-election/.

AP News. "Transcript of Trump's Speech at Rally before US Capitol Riot." January 13, 2021. https://apnews.com/article/election-2020-joe-biden-donald-trump-capitol-siege-media-e79eb5164613d6718e9f4502eb471f27.

Bencks, Jarred. "Trump and the Language of Insurrection." *BrandeisNOW*, January 12, 2021. www.brandeis.edu/now/2021/january/trump-language-capitol-riot-mcintosh.html.

Ben-Ghiat, Ruth. *Strongmen: Mussolini to the Present*. New York: W. W. Norton & Company, 2020.

Billeaud, Jacques. "Man Who Wore Horns, Hat Apologizes for Storming Capitol." *AP News*, February 9, 2021. https://apnews.com/article/jacob-chansley-apologizes-capitol-riot-66760ebdffe55ea2d9b99965288d80ff.

Blackwell, Christopher W. "The Development of Athenian Democracy," in Adriaan Lanni, ed., "Athenian Law in its Democratic Context" (Center for Hellenic Studies On-line Discussion Series). Republished in C.W. Blackwell, ed., Dēmos: Classical Athenian Democracy (A. Mahoney and R. Scaife, eds., The Stoa: A Consortium for Electronic Publication in the Humanities [www.stoa.org]) edition of January 24, 2003.

Braund, Susanna, and Glenn W. Most. *Ancient Anger: Perspectives from Homer to Galen*. Cambridge: Cambridge University Press, 2007.

Burns, Timothy. "Anger in Thucydides and Aristophanes: The Case of Cleon." In *The Political Theory of Aristophanes: Explorations in Poetic Wisdom*, edited by Jeremy Mhire and Bryan-Paul Frost. Albany: SUNY Press, 2014.

Cathey, Libby, and Meghan Keneally. "A Look Back at Trump Comments Perceived by Some as Inciting Violence." *ABC News*, May 30, 2020. https://abcnews.go.com/Politics/back-trump-comments-perceived-encouraging-violence/story?id=48415766.

Cavna, Michael. "The Comedy that Got Inside Trump's Head." *The Washington Post*, September 22, 2020. www.washingtonpost.com/arts-entertainment/2020/09/22/trump-comedy-satire-humor-best/.

Chua, Amy. "The Constitution is Threatened by Tribalism." *The Atlantic*, October 2018. www.theatlantic.com/magazine/archive/2018/10/the-threat-of-tribalism/568342/.

Cineas, Fabiola. "Donald Trump is the Accelerant." *Vox*, updated January 9, 2021. www.vox.com/21506029/trump-violence-tweets-racist-hate-speech.

Cusher, Brent Edwin. "Thucydides on Innovative Leadership and its Limits." *The Political Science Reviewer* 44, no. 2 (2020): 327–352. https://politicalsciencereviewer.wisc.edu/index.php/psr/article/view/635.

Dobsky, Bernard. "Democracy, Demagogues, and Political Wisdom: Understanding Trump in the Wake of Thucydides' History." In *Trump and Political Philosophy*, edited by Angel Jaramillo Torres and Mark Sable, 75–92. Cham, CH: Palgrave Macmillan, 2018.

Duhigg, Charles. "The Real Roots of American Rage." *The Atlantic*, January/February 2019. www.theatlantic.com/magazine/archive/2019/01/charles-duhigg-american-anger/576424/.

The Editors of Encyclopaedia Britannica. "Deus Ex Machina." *Encyclopedia Britannica*, March 20, 2020. www.britannica.com/art/deus-ex-machina.

Encarnación, Omar G. "American Caudillo: Trump and the Latin-Americanization of U.S. Politics." *Foreign Affairs*, May 12, 2020. www.foreignaffairs.com/articles/united-states/2016-05-12/american-caudillo.

Fallows, James. "Reporter's Notebook." *The Atlantic*, May 4, 2020. www.theatlantic.com/notes/.

Farivar, Masood. "Capitol Riot Exposed QAnon's Violent Potential." *VOA News*, March 31, 2021. www.voanews.com/usa/capitol-riot-exposed-qanons-violent-potential.

Harrison, Kellie L. "The Forgotten Center: An Analysis into the Disappearing Moderate in a Climate of Increasing Political Polarization." *Inquiries Journal* 12, no. 9 (2020). www.inquiriesjournal.com/a?id=1796.

Hennessey, Susan, and Benjamin Wittes. *Unmaking the Presidency: Donald Trump's War on the World's Most Powerful Office*. New York: Farrar, Straus and Giroux, 2020.

Horgan, John. "The Plague at Athens, 430–427 BCE." *World History Encyclopedia*, August 24, 2016. www.ancient.eu/article/939/.

Kagan, Donald. *Pericles of Athens and the Birth of Democracy*. New York: The Free Press, 1991.

Kalimtzis, Kostas. *Taming Anger: The Hellenic Approach to the Limitations of Reason*. London: Bloomsbury Academic, 2012.

Kaufman, Scott. "Donald Trump's Real Ambition." *Scientific American*, July 24, 2016. https://blogs.scientificamerican.com/beautiful-minds/donald-trump-s-real-ambition/.

Konstan, David. "Affect and Emotion in Greek Literature." *Oxford Handbooks Online*, October 2015. doi:10.1093/oxfordhb/9780199935390.013.41.

Lane, Melissa. "The Origins of the Statesman—Demagogue Distinction in and after Ancient Athens." *Journal of the History of Ideas* 73, no. 2 (2012): 179–200. doi:10.1353/jhi.2012.0020.

Last, Jonathan. *What to Expect When No One's Expecting: America's Coming Demographic Disaster*. New York: Encounter Books, 2014.

Madison, James. "Federalist No. 10." In *The Federalist Papers*. New York: New York Daily Advertiser, November 22, 1787.

McGill, Andrew. "Out of Every 10 Trump Supporters, Nine Are White." *The Atlantic*, September 14, 2016. www.theatlantic.com/politics/archive/2016/09/dissecting-donald-trumps-support/499739/.

Menaldo, Mark. "American Barbarism." *The Constitutionalist*, February 1, 2021. https://theconstitutionalist.org/2021/02/01/american-barbarism-by-mark-antonio-menaldo/.

Menaldo, Mark. "Barack Obama's Foreign Policy Leadership: Renewing America's Image." In *American Identity in the Age of Obama*, edited by Amílcar Antonio Barreto and Richard L. O'Bryant, 212–235. New York: Routledge, 2013.

Menaldo, Mark. *Leadership and Transformative Ambition in International Relations*. Cheltenham, UK: Edward Elgar Publishing, 2013.

Obama, Barack. *News Conference*, The White House, Washington, DC, April 4, 2009.

Orwin, Clifford. *The Humanity of Thucydides*. Princeton, NJ: Princeton University Press, 1994.

Pew Research Center. "Partisanship and Political Animosity in 2016." June 22, 2016. www.pewresearch.org/politics/2016/06/22/partisanship-and-political-animosity-in-2016/.

Romano, Andrew. "How Does Obama Woo 'Downscale Dems'?" *Newsweek*, August 15, 2007. www.newsweek.com/how-does-obama-woo-downscale-dems-99139.

Rosenthal, Max J. "The Trump Files: Donald Perfectly Explains Why He Doesn't Have a Presidential Temperament." *Mother Jones*, July 6, 2020. www.motherjones.com/2020-elections/2020/07/trump-files-donald-perfectly-explains-why-he-doesnt-have-presidential-temperament/.

Rucker, Phillip, Parker Ashley, and Josh Dawsey. "After Inciting Mob Attack, Trump Retreats in Rage. Then, Grudgingly, He Admits His Loss." *Washington Post*, January 7, 2021. www.washingtonpost.com/politics/trump-rage-riot/2021/01/07/26894c54-5108-1eb-b96e-0e54447b23a1_story.html.

Sargent, Greg. "Donald Trump's Revealing Quote about 'American Exceptionalism'." *Washington Post*, June 7, 2016. www.washingtonpost.com/blogs/plum-line/wp/2016/06/07/donald-trumps-revealing-quote-about-american-exceptionalism/.

Sullivan, Andrew. "America Wasn't Built for Humans." *New York Magazine*, September 18, 2017. https://nymag.com/intelligencer/2017/09/can-democracy-survive-tribalism.html.

Time Staff. "Donald Trump's Presidential Announcement Speech." June 16, 2015. https://time.com/3923128/donald-trump-announcement-speech/.

Trump, Donald. "Mount Rushmore Speech," Keystone, SD, July 3, 2020.

Uscinski, Joseph E. *Conspiracy Theories and the People Who Believe Them*. New York: Oxford University Press, 2018.

Washington Post. "The Fact Checker's Database." updated January 20, 2021. www.washingtonpost.com/graphics/politics/trump-claims-database/.

4

PLATO'S TYRANT AND DONALD TRUMP'S (IN)AUTHENTIC LEADERSHIP[1]

Alfonso Vergaray

What is it about former President Donald Trump that explains his appeal? Common opinion points to his unconventional style. Unlike his political opponents, Trump "tells it like it is" and appears willing to do whatever it takes to achieve his ends. That style led some observers to claim that Trump's authenticity, or at least the perception of his authenticity, best explains his popularity and staying power.[2] Indeed, that is a fair assessment. I add to that general sensibility the claim that Trump's indiscriminate pushing of boundaries (i.e., his "authentic" style) mirrors a tyrant-like style that provides a useful lens to consider his ability to gain and maintain support. In particular, I look to the tyrant in Plato's *Republic* to consider whether Trump's soul is tyrannical in a Platonic sense. Trump does not perfectly reflect the tyrant in the *Republic*, nor do I claim that he is a tyrant in any other comprehensive sense. Plato's claim that the tyrant, for example, places his subjects in absolute slavery and reduces them to fear, poverty, and misery (577c—578a) does not fit Trump.[3] Still, the disordered soul of the tyrant, the core characteristic of Plato's tyrant, does correspond with Trump's character.[4] Tyranny, for Plato, is a disorder of the soul in which the passions enslave and rule the higher part of the soul. Like the tyrant, Trump's disordered soul leads him to pay little heed to the legal and social norms that restrain most individuals.[5] Trump's perennial entanglements with the law and his boorish style of politicking evince his unrestrained tyrant-like style, which is an expression of extreme freedom. Freedom, Plato asserts, is the guiding principle in a democracy, and when a democratic people define freedom as having no restraints, a figure such as Trump finds a captive audience. While a sizable segment of Trump's followers value restraints in certain contexts—to the extent that their calls for "law and order," restoring religious or cultural norms, and the like reflect their values—their leader, Trump, the disorderly, often unhinged, tyrant-like leader,

DOI: 10.4324/9781003110361-4

is willing to challenge almost any legal or social norm to achieve his ends. Plato provides insight into why and how this sort of figure appeals to democratic citizens awestruck by what they incorrectly perceive as an authentically free leader.[6]

Understanding Trump's appeal in the United States—the emblematic democracy in modern times—helps alert friends of democracy to the possible rise of tyrant-like figures in the future. This chapter examines one aspect of Trump's appeal through an analysis of the most pronounced feature of his personality—his erratic, convention-bending style—to offer a broad account of Trump's appeal as an authentic leader. This analysis abstracts from particulars[7] to make an observation about broader dynamics, namely, the relationship between democracy, democratic citizens, freedom, and leader preferences. More specifically, it takes seriously Plato's contention that democracy, tyranny, and the tyrant are intimately interconnected. Democracies, like all regimes, according to Plato, breakdown, and understanding the tyrant as a political opportunist[8] is key to discerning its unraveling.

I first connect Trump's popularity before, during, and after his presidency (2016–2021) to the aura of authenticity he projected. I then turn to books eight and nine of Plato's *Republic* to examine the tyrant and tyranny in relation to democracy. While I stick closely to the text in my reading of the *Republic*, I also use creative license in my interpretations to bring out parallels between Plato's tyrant and Trump. A critic might look skeptically on a work that attempts to use an ancient text to shed light on contemporary matters, pointing, for instance, to the dangers of conflating ancient democracy and liberty with its modern iterations.[9] Although such dangers are certainly present, I contend that Plato's analysis of liberty and democracy can fruitfully, albeit imperfectly, be lifted beyond the confines of ancient Greece.[10] I conclude arguing that an embrace of extreme freedom, which makes the tyrant appealing to democratic citizens, can be tempered by cultivating a dedication to civic equality.

Trump's Popularity

Despite the former president's popularity with many Americans, by various quantifiable measures, Trump was an unpopular president. In the 2016 presidential election, Trump lost the popular vote by 2.8 million votes.[11] Four years later, in 2020, with a voter turnout of 67%—higher than that of any other presidential election since 1901—Trump lost by over seven million votes.[12] Trump's job-approval ratings, which barely reached 50% in his four years in office and ended at an all-time low, also tell the story of a deeply unpopular president.[13] Still, by other measures, Trump was persistently popular. His popularity among his followers remained constant and grew over time. As a nominee in the 2016 presidential primary, Trump received more votes in a contest for the Republican presidential nomination than anyone on record.[14] In 2020, he received the most votes ever by a sitting president.[15] Trump not only tapped into the Tea Party wing of the Republican Party but also flipped previously leaning Democratic areas and awakened a dormant electorate to the Republican side. Trump's ability to command the American public's attention no doubt helped drive the 2020 presidential election's record-high voter turnout. That election, consequently, served more as a referendum on Trump rather than a contest against his opponent, Joe Biden, or the Democratic Party. Admiration for Trump also peaked immediately following the 2020 election: according to a Gallup poll, Americans considered Trump to be the country's most admired man.[16] While his support took a blow in the immediate aftermath of the attack on the US Capitol, it quickly rebounded among a sizable segment of the Republican electorate and party leadership. In short, while Trump was not a popular president in terms of the raw numbers of Americans supporting him, his ability to maintain support and to draw attention to his presidency was unmatched.

Trump's ability to attract attention with his erratic behavior brought questions about his personality to the forefront in his presidential contests. This was most evident in a common refrain heard from prospective Trump voters in the 2020 election: "I support Trump's policies," went the first part of the refrain, followed by the inevitable qualification, "but I disapprove of his wild behavior/tweeting."[17] Such statements reflect ambivalence about supporting, on the one hand, an uncivil leader and, on the other hand, supporting policies and aims Trump's hesitant followers endorsed or at least found to be more palatable than those offered by his Democratic opponents. Focusing on Trump's policies, however, was nearly impossible, given his bombastic personality, which overshadowed his policy proposals. Trump came across as obviously rude, immature, and inappropriate, someone you wouldn't want your children emulating. From a different angle, Trump's unpleasantries appeared to be an amusing show, a gravity-defying stunt demanding attention. Both sides of the Trump coin are interrelated insofar as what disturbs can elicit intrigue. As keen observers of human behavior have long recognized, "sometimes we are perversely attracted to people whom we actually loathe."[18] I suspect that aside from diehard loyalists who loved everything about Trump, including his erratic personality, others—perhaps even those who fought against him fervently—harbored simultaneous feelings of amusement and disgust toward him. So, what is it about Trump that disturbs yet entices?

Trump's personality takes freedom, arguably the most precious commodity in a democracy, and embodies it in its most vulgar manifestation. In other words, Trump projects a free life, with freedom understood in this context as doing as one likes without restraint. Trump appeared to say what he wanted and did what he pleased, signaling a free and authentic life.[19] Neither "political correctness" nor any form of political decorum held him back. Trump's informal antics resonated with his followers and distinguished him from his political opponents who in contrast appeared inauthentic in their stilted speech and manners.[20]

The association of unrestrained freedom with authenticity has a history that predates the Trump presidency. Authenticity is part of a broader Western tradition that traces its roots to Socrates and that eventually blossomed in the modern period—what some scholars have called an "age of authenticity".[21] It corresponds with "an ethic of autonomy" that emphasizes and values an individual's self-making capabilities.[22] In highly stratified societies, in which social and individual mobility are severely limited, individuals stepping outside their rigid roles in an expression of authenticity would be perceived as an aberration, as they would be breaking the norms at the center of collective life. Valuing other goods above freedom—such as military valor, honor, and divine right—those cultures would view authenticity as at best a subordinate good. Yet in free societies that celebrate individual autonomy (i.e., democracies), the authentic individual finds a home in which she is admired for her ability to be true to herself. Consider slogans popular in American culture, that citadel of freedom: "Follow your heart," "Do your own thing," "Be yourself," and the like. In a different cultural context, "doing your own thing" would be anything but admirable. Instead, it might appear undisciplined or disloyal to a cherished way of life.[23]

In the 2016 presidential election cycle, authenticity was at the forefront of public discussion, with some calling the race "the authenticity election."[24] In that election, Trump was perceived as the most authentic candidate by far, first during the Republican primary and then in the presidential race against his Democratic opponent, former Secretary of State Hillary Clinton. While the search for an authentic president is nothing new,[25] it took on added features with Trump. To what is usually associated with authenticity, namely being genuine in a relatable way, Trump added a crass, unapologetic bravado that gave voice to his followers' pent-up resentments, delivering to them incivility with a cause. His political rivals set a different tone, coming across as rehearsed and self-restrained; your quintessential politicians. The 2020 presidential election cycle saw a continuation of Trump as the standard-bearer of authenticity. Ivanka Trump highlighted her father's authenticity in that election when she juxtaposed his Democratic opponent, Joe Biden, as "a vessel for whatever the fringe of the party or the mainstream media want to be," as compared to her father, who she claimed was "arguably the most authentic president we've ever had."[26]

The assertion that Trump is authentic might strike some as odd.[27] Rather than authentic, certain observers saw him as a staged act (e.g., a salesman,[28] self-help guru,[29] or demagogue) who lacks self-understanding. In Platonic terms, he has a disordered soul, ruled by his passions instead of reason. Indeed, as I explain later, there is little substance behind Trump's authentically free façade. That said, the perception of authenticity is what matters when describing leader–follower dynamics. A democratic audience who embraces a corrupt or, as Plato put it, "extreme" conception of freedom can *perceive* a Trump-like character as free and authentic. Follower perception alone, in other words, determines the meaning of authenticity when everyday practices are evaluated.

Plato's *Republic*

Plato's *Republic* is a dialogue on justice, education, politics, and philosophy. The unifying feature of those themes is Plato's preoccupation with the polar opposition between the tyrannical (corrupt) soul and the well-ordered soul. That tension between two extremes, the worst and the best, is arguably the overarching focus of the dialogue.[30] At one end of that pole is Socrates' development, in conversation with his interlocutors, of the ideal city. A central feature of the ideal city is its perfectly ordered nature, reflected in the differentiated roles taken on by the city's inhabitants. The city's inhabitants also reflect that perfect order within themselves as well-balanced rational, spirited, and appetitive souls. Book eight of the *Republic* introduces four inferior regime types: timocracy, oligarchy, democracy, and tyranny. Those regimes lacking the perfect harmony found in the ideal city, organically and cyclically transition around the ideal city. An understanding of the animating principle/desire driving the disharmony within each city clarifies the transitions among inferior cities, with tyranny representing the worst of the cities.

The insatiable desire to become as rich as possible, for example, characterizes an oligarchy (555b9–10). That desire leads to its downfall, as the insatiable drive toward riches drowns out a concern for virtue and honor, leaving the door open to intemperance. Consequently, the wealthy—caught as they are in money-seeking intemperance (555c1–5)—financially exploit the youth. The transition to democracy occurs when the poor take note of the weakened and gluttonous oligarchs in power and then decide collectively to overrun them, installing democratic rule in its place (556c7–e1).

So, what is a democracy like, and what sort of person inhabits a democracy? A democracy is "full of freedom and freedom of speech," Socrates suggests to Ademinatus. Its emphasis on liberty leads "each person [to] arrange his own life in whatever way pleases him" (557b9). Democracies have, in other words, great flexibility and tolerance for diverse ways of living. In Socrates' terms, it "contains all kinds of constitutions" (557d2). Democracies contain timocratic, oligarchic, and other types of people who are found in other regimes. That diversity leads Socrates to describe democracy as "the most beautiful of all the constitutions"; it is like "an embroidered cloak with every kind of ornament" (557c3). That beauty is courtesy of the freedom at the center of democratic regimes. And it is the very emphasis on freedom that, in democracy's nadir, leads to an embrace of "extreme freedom" and to democracy's eventual downfall.[31]

In the mindset of extreme freedom, citizens understand any restraint as an infringement. As a consequence, they develop "sensitive" souls, "so that if anyone tries to impose the least degree of slavery, they get irritated and cannot bear it"

(563d5). Plato's encounters with democratic citizens in his time undoubtedly influenced his thoughts on how democratic citizens think of freedom. Impressively, his insights have carried over to democracies in the present day. Consider former New York City Mayor Mike Bloomberg's campaign to fight obesity, which included a ban on drinks that contain excessive sugar. Politicians and others decried, in a panic, the threat of "big government" and "the nanny state," which in general expressed their dismay at a potential loss of freedom represented by the ban. Freedom crusaders united to protect the precious right to drink 7–11's Big Gulp.[32] Similarly, during the Covid-19 pandemic, protestors resisted and demonstrated against mask requirements that they claimed were an infringement on their freedom.[33] As an exasperated epidemiologist, Eli Perencevich, noted when discussing anti-maskers at the beginning of the pandemic in the United States, "We've decided as a society that we're going to take all the people in our healthcare system and pummel them because we have some insane idea about what freedom really is."[34] Introducing a new law in a society that values freedom, as illustrated in the previous examples, awakens sensitive souls who see any hint of restraint as a sign of tyranny.

And so it goes that as democracy begins to embrace a radical conception of freedom, the people start using that conceptual frame as a reference to understand their lives. This newfound attitude threatens the legitimacy of written and unwritten laws, as democratic citizens interpret legal and social norms as threats to their freedom. All authority and hierarchy become suspect. By not prizing any particular way of life, a democracy, Socrates observes, ends up "assigning a sort of equality to equals and unequals alike" (558c4). The relationship between teacher and student, and parent and child, for example, become blurred. "The son," he observes, "gets into the habit of behaving like a father, feeling neither shame nor fear in front of his parents—all in order to be *free*" (562e7). Slowly, this disregard for traditional authorities broadly permeates social relations, threatening the laws and norms that govern human society. Still, laws and social norms are not immediately thrown aside. The fear of social ostracism and/or legal punishments is enough to restrain most. The desire to break free from restraints, however, remains, albeit restricted to daydreams and fantasies. So the democratic person goes about his or her life in tension, imagining and desiring a free life, while stopping short of living that life out of (prudent) fear.

As a desire for radical freedom takes hold among the people in a democracy, the tyrant has an entry point to appeal to their sensibilities. He embodies the unencumbered pursuit of insatiable desire, bringing the people's fantasies of unrestricted freedom to life. In upending the social and legal laws in a democracy, the tyrant leads a democracy to its eventual downfall (562b9–c2). Still, the lawless, bestial character of the tyrant is not an *ex nihilo* occurrence peculiar to the tyrant. Socrates makes clear that that character is present in every individual, manifested in his or her dream life, even by those "who seem to be entirely moderate" (571b–72b; see also Laws 697ac). Consequently, any reflection on the tyrant should include a reflection on the tyrannical elements found in all humans.

Consider an infant. The infant demands that his or her desires be met without consideration for others. In the pursuit of fulfilling desire, the infant wakes up in the middle of the night and appears to say, "I don't care that you are asleep, feed me!" or, at other moments, "I want to be held! No matter that you are busy. Hold me!" Any parent is well acquainted with the infant as a self-absorbed narcissist. The infant becomes "His Majesty, the Baby," as Freud observed in his essay "On Narcissism."[35] During this stage, humans first experience frustrated desires, no matter how good their caretakers are. The pursuit of desires, of course, does not end in infancy. Later, as the cognitive faculties develop, the frustration accompanying unfulfilled desires can inflame the imagination. When people experience a frustrated desire for food, they might begin to imagine the food that they craved, as an approximation of that thwarted desire. That is a relatively harmless instance of the interplay between frustration and desire. Desires, however, are far from libertarian; they do not end "where another man's nose begins." They do not stop, in other words, when they are about to interfere with the well-being of others. The person who is single-mindedly focused on acquiring wealth, for example, ignores that her pursuit harms others. When such a mindset takes over a society at large, the very stability of the social order is placed in jeopardy, as Socrates illustrates in his discussion on oligarchies. Or consider a man who jealously desires a beloved and feels an uncontrollable urge to possess her. The consequences can be dire. The endless homicides committed as "crimes of passion" are a dark reminder of desires run amok. Humans, in short, need to be taught to restrain their desires, to deal with the frustrations that are part of being a desiring creature. Laws and punishments, whether legal, social, or religious in nature, are necessary to remind the tyrant in all of us of the repercussions that await if we give into our darker angels.[36]

Unlike the many in a democracy, the tyrant unequivocally gives into his desires. He doesn't hold back. He says what's on his mind. He behaves erratically, not to be restrained by any law, convention, or individual. He has "in his soul the greatest and strongest tyrant of all" (575c–d). Tired of fakes, a democratic audience drunk on an extreme conception of freedom sees the tyrant as the most authentic leader. They view the tyrant's shamelessness and lack of moderation as assets,[37] juxtaposed with the inauthentic style of his opponents. The tyrant is a dream come to life, as he lives out the fantasies of ordinary citizens who wish they too could to live their lives without restraint.[38]

In this sense, Trump resembles the tyrant in the *Republic*. To those embracing a radical conception of freedom Trump is the embodiment of an authentically free individual. He speaks and acts as he pleases, appearing fearless, quashing his political opponents and the norms they dared not transgress. Who precisely is this tyrant that Trump resembles? Etymologically, the tyrant (*tyrannos*) is a leader who lacks links to an ancestral past, unbound from the norms and laws of a shared history. Trump is not unique in that sense, as the chapters in this volume demonstrate. Still, to the public imaginary of the 2016 electorate, he appeared "new," given that no viable presidential candidate in their memory resembled Trump's style. They experienced him, in other words, as "coming out of nowhere." More particularly, in the ancient and Platonic conception, the tyrant is "a monster of desire."[39] He is "chaos incarnate."[40] Trump's chaotic style was no secret; it was legion in the Trump White House and on his Twitter feed. The quintessential instance of Trump unleashed occurred during the attack on the Capitol on January 6, 2021. An unnamed Trump official described him that day as "a total monster."[41] Not only did Trump take a largely passive attitude when calling off his supporters from a volatile situation that turned violent,[42] with a number of rioters calling for the death of lawmakers,[43] when he finally addressed the mob, he continued emphasizing his fantastical claim the election was "fraudulent," concluding his message by telling those who had forcefully attacked the Capitol that they were loved and "very special."[44] A warped display of a man out of control.

> "Perhaps," a critic might reply. "Trump may resemble the man you portray, but that hardly makes him a tyrant! Trump was not a murderous leader who 'constantly stir[red] up war,' as Socrates claims a tyrant would (565e2 & 566e6). Instead, he largely stood against the military wing of the Republican party. Trump was more bravado than anything. For example, he may have called the fight against COVID-19 a 'war.' Still, in the end, even when presented with a golden opportunity to consolidate power, he instead chose to rely on a federalist approach. No emergency powers were used. A state of exception was not enacted.[45] So much for your tyrant. And to the mob, Trump showed restraint! He could have ordered his followers to fight to the death, as would a proper tyrant (565e3). In his four years in office, his unconventional style may have displeased many, but that alone hardly makes him a tyrant."

As I conceded at the outset of this chapter, Trump is not a perfect image of Plato's tyrant. It is his tyrant-like disordered soul, manifested in his explosive and unpredictable nature, which corresponds with Plato's tyrant. As a complete tyrant in Plato's mold, however, Trump occupies a gray space, as he does in many areas. Trump bends and tests boundaries without exactly bursting past them, thereby creating enough ambiguity to allow multiple interpretations for his actions.[46] Even in speech, Trump equivocates in ways that allow listeners to hear what they please, giving his detractors and followers supporting "evidence" for their respective views.[47] He frequently stated, for example, that his administration had the Covid-19 virus "under control," and that the virus is "not under control for any place in the world."[48] Sometimes, however, Trump's actions moved beyond murky gray skies to clearer daylight. Take Robert Paxton's evolving views of Trump as fascist. Paxton, an expert on fascism who has written, studied, and reflected on the meaning and history of fascism for decades, resisted labeling Trump a fascist for most of Trump's tenure as president. There were telltale signs, he noted, but Trump was not a fascist when considering the totality of his (in)actions. "Trump's incitement of the invasion of the Capitol," however, changed Paxton's views. The label of fascist "now seems," Paxton wrote a few days after the invasion, "not just acceptable but necessary."[49] Much like the case of Trump as fascist before January 6, 2021, Trump's tyrant-like character captures the spirit of Plato's tyrant without precisely embodying it.[50]

The spirit of the tyrant is found in his unregulated desires that correspond with the extreme freedom embraced by democratic citizens. When describing the tyrant, Socrates notes, "Passion lives like a tyrant within him in complete anarchy and lawlessness" (575a). Trump possesses his own form of lawlessness. Consider the little over four thousand lawsuits Trump amassed in four decades, most of which predate his time in office.[51] The bulk of those cases represent Trump's attempts to skirt the law, which over time have contributed to his invincible image. As Jim Zirin, a former prosecutor for the Southern District of New York, observed, "I think [Trump] thinks of himself as the Teflon man—that no one can touch him, that he has absolutely no accountability."[52] That attitude was in part cultivated by his early collaboration with lawyer Roy Cohn. Cohn was fond of saying cynically, "fuck the law, who's the judge?"[53] He told *Penthouse* that he decided "long ago to make my own rules."[54] "What attracted [Trump] to Roy Cohn," said Sidney Zion, a reporter who worked with Cohn on his autobiography, "was here was someone who had beaten the system."[55] Trump's ability to beat the system, to do as he pleased without consequence, is part of his appeal. Or as Zirin puts it, "There's a certain American romance to getting away with it. We all secretly admire the guy that can."[56] In this way, Trump fed into the fantasies of those longing for the kind of freedom only a tyrant can possess.

Notice that a Trump-like leader appeals to a segment of democratic citizens who fear they are losing, or have lost, power.[57] They feel, in other words, the most restrained from a lack or loss of social status, opportunity, and/or wealth.[58] Those restraints, in turn, make them feel subject to powers that are beyond their control (e.g., the deep state, gentry liberalism, and so on). Embracing an unrestrained (free) leader gives them the possibility to get back at the system—giving it the proverbial middle finger—and provides them with the slightest hope that they can reshape the country to their liking.[59] The tyrant-like leader represents their last hurrah, a final gamble to save a nation they feel is on the brink of collapse.[60] While chaos and disorder are the hallmarks of the tyrant's behavior, his supporters see glimmers of virtue as the tyrant courageously stands up against their enemies.[61] For those who revel in the status quo, fearing neither loss of power or status, an unrestrained leader lacks appeal. They can, after all, exploit their resources and connections within a democracy to live as they please as private citizens. Consequently, a portion of those elites will see the tyrant as a threat to their way of life, as he threatens the lifestyle they are perfectly equipped to exploit. Another portion who do not find the tyrant appealing might nonetheless create alliances with him to further their hold on power.[62]

The tyrant, of course, is not moved by the desires or wishes of his followers or critics.[63] He is in it for himself. Paradoxically, the tyrant who is glaringly in it for himself convinces his most fervent followers that he is in it for them. Intoxicated by what they perceive as an authentically free leader, they are blinded to the slavery they are setting themselves up for. "For extreme freedom," Socrates notes, "probably cannot lead to anything but a change to extreme slavery, whether in a private individual or city" (564a3). Extreme slavery, in Plato's telling, is a condition in which an individual or city is enslaved to the unnecessary appetites and passions. In that condition, the rational part of the soul is subordinate to the whims of desire. The tyrant represents the bridge from extreme freedom (in the late stages of democracy) to extreme slavery (tyranny). When the tyrant, with his wild and unpredictable style, first appears to a democratic public, the people are convinced that he is the freest individual. Trump had that act down. His chaotic style was the hallmark of his administration. His displays of outrageousness were mistaken for authenticity, as his spontaneous behavior sent a message to the demos: "Here is a leader who is subject to no one and does as he pleases."

Consider, however, that outrageousness is often a defense against authenticity. It masks, in the artificial shell of outrageousness, vulnerability. It was perhaps to be expected that Trump struggled as consoler in chief.[64] His strong suit was never being vulnerable and empathetic. Instead, Trump excels at being on a stage, putting on a show, from "The Apprentice" to the White House.[65] The authentic self hides behind the show. Contrary to outrageousness, authenticity sometimes, perhaps even most of the time, requires one to be ordinary.[66] That mode of being may not garner attention, but it is closer to the authentic self than to the outrageous self. Arising from the freest regime, the outrageously self-absorbed tyrant simultaneously enslaves himself and the city. "So, those with a tyrannical nature," Socrates observes, "live their entire lives without ever being friends with anyone[,] . . . never getting a taste of freedom or true friendship" (576a3). The tyrant, in sum, is neither free nor authentic. His disordered soul guides his actions, leaving him, in the end, enslaved and in solitude. Trump is not perfectly captured in Plato's tyrant, but he is perilously close, giving the nation a taste of a tyrant-like leader.

Conclusion

If the principle of tyranny is the implicit aim of freedom, how might democracies avoid that fate? Put differently, what might temper the appeal of tyrant-like leaders in free societies? Following Wilson Carey McWilliams, I suggest that in a democracy, a love of equality, rightly understood, tempers a love of freedom.[67] In tempering freedom, a love of equality does not destroy freedom; it perfects it, facilitating the stability and longevity of a free society.

Equality, like freedom, is indispensable to democracies. More particularly, having an equal share in rule—political equality—is a necessary condition for democratic governance. As Aristotle argued, majority rule derives from political equality, which he described as ruling and being ruled in turn (1317b3). Equal share in ruling informs majority rule, as it implores the majority to listen respectfully to and to consider minority opinions. That respect, in turn, points to the importance of civic equality, an "equal feeling and sympathy, a conviction of equal dignity and common destiny."[68] Equality thus understood moves citizens to consider themselves in relation to others and serves as a reminder that each individual is part of a larger whole.

Freedom, quite differently, points inward to the individual, and, in its many iterations, it is "engrossed with limits and power."[69] To achieve freedom, individuals must fight against some power, or someone, that stands in the way of their freedom. Freedom seeks to overcome all limits, including limits derived from public and private relations. A society in love with freedom, and that neglects political and civic equality, leaves itself exposed to a narrowly self-interested populace that loses sight of equal dignity and common destiny. Put differently, without a society's embrace of political and civic equality, the undemocratic idea of freedom as "living as you like" without restraints (i.e., extreme freedom) takes hold.[70]

A remedy to such an outcome is a proper schooling in political and civic equality. This is especially relevant given the fragility of relying solely on a representative form of governance and the separation of powers that were designed to restrain the mob in modern constitutional democracies.[71] Such an education would remind citizens, for example, that in democracies, unity does not mean unity of opinion. Understanding that rule is shared, democratic citizens accept different political outcomes. The vast majority of the political policies advocated by Trump and his supporters, for instance, are legitimate alternatives in a democracy.[72] It is a mistake to think otherwise. Opponents of those views might argue that some of Trump's policies are unconstitutional, or they might object that they are un-American. Perhaps. One should not lose sight, however, that Republicans (Trumpians) say the same about certain policies advocated by Democrats. Instead of a zero-sum outlook regarding partisan political alternatives, the overarching sentiment in a democracy should be of civic equality. An uncivil outlook would insist that only one political outcome is legitimate, and it would fight for its victory no matter the cost.[73] Trump, of course, displayed marks of incivility throughout his presidency, culminating in his rejection of the 2020 presidential election results, striking at the heart of the democratic process.

An example of civic mindfulness during an election defeat is found in former Vice President Al Gore's concession speech in the 2000 presidential election.

In that election, Florida's electoral ballots were contested, leading to weeks of battle, first in the Florida Supreme Court, and then culminating in the US Supreme Court. Gore conceded after the Supreme Court's decision granting the election to George Bush. In his concession speech, he stated, "Let there be no doubt, while I strongly disagree with the court's decision, I accept it. I accept the finality of this outcome." Gore went on to explain that the outcome of the election had "ended, resolved, as it must be resolved, through the honored institutions of our democracy." Having "strongly disagreed" with the court's outcome, Gore could have claimed that partisanship was at work in the Supreme Court's decision and that that decision, unless corrected, would lead to the illegitimate presidency of his opponent. Instead, Gore stressed that "partisan feeling must yield to patriotism," which in Gore's case called for a gracious concession.[74] Gore paid heed, in other words, to civic and political equality, placing the common good above narrow self-interest.

The act of putting aside partisanship for the sake common good is not limited to one political party. It is hard to find a greater supporter of Trump than his former Vice President Mike Pence. Yet, it was Pence who steadfastly refused to follow Trump's request—amid death threats and enormous pressure—to bypass his duty to certify the 2020 election results. Even the riotous events of January 6th did not shake Pence's resolve. Following the attack on the Capitol Pence said that he will "always be proud that we did our part, on that tragic day, to reconvene the Congress and fulfill our duty under the Constitution and the laws of the United States."[75] On that day, Pence's loyalty to the Constitution and laws of the United Stated trumped his loyalty to the President.

Pence and Gore's example, while important lessons for political leaders,[76] do not speak directly to the fragmented partisan rancor that infects American politics. Partisanship and a fragmented public are, to be sure, nothing new in American political history. Still, today's fragmented and deeply partisan public have their twenty-first-century peculiarities. Most poignantly, information technologies have altered the public square. With every year that passes, more of the public integrate their online habits and communities with their offline lives, blurring the boundary between the online and offline.[77] Once-obscure forms of communication tucked away at the edges of the Internet have gravitated into everyday forms of political communication.[78] Meanwhile, the algorithms that drive social media usage confirm users' individual biases, resulting in "echo chambers" that further divide the public.[79] A good share of those echo chambers, in turn, spread virulent conspiracy theories at an exponential rate, amplifying fridge ideas to everyday realities.

In these conditions, we need fresh thinking about old political puzzles. How do you foster in the public a conviction of equal dignity and the common good? How do you create a sense of public spiritedness that combats narrow self-interest? What are the national narratives needed to facilitate holding together America's increasingly unwieldy union?[80] It is the task of the current generation to consider these perennial political puzzles in light of new circumstances. All of these challenges, in one way or another, require restoring civic equality, which in turn demands a reckoning with the oligarchic impulses in American politics that place profit and wealth above democratic values. As was highlighted in this chapter, a democracy's failure to cultivate political and civic equality leaves an opening for the tyrant to exploit the public's embrace of extreme freedom. The tyrant loses his luster, however, when faced with a civically minded public who see their fellow citizens as friends, or at least as an approximation of friends, ruling in turn.[81] Liberty is not endangered by a civically minded public. It is enhanced: "Liberty, in an ancient paradox, to be perfected, must be *ruled* by the common good and the good life."[82]

Notes

1 Thanks are due to John Charles, Michael Harvey, Seth Jaffe, Mark A. Menaldo, and Erin W-M Meyer. Earlier versions of this chapter were presented at the 2018 annual conference of the International Leadership Association and the 2020 Midwest Seminar in Ancient and Medieval Philosophy.

2 See Alexandra Hutzler, "Donald Trump Is 'Perhaps the Most Authentic President Ever, Despite Constantly Saying Things That Aren't True, Former White House Aide Cliff Sims Says," *Time*, January 1, 2019, https://www.newsweek.com/former-white-house-aide-calls-trump-most-authentic-president-1311447. Adam Garfinkle writes that "Trump is in the Oval Office in large part because he seems authentic." Adam Garfinkle, "Trump the Authentic," *American Interest*, January 14, 2018, https://www.the-american-interest.com/2018/01/14/trump-the-authentic. See also Oliver Hahl, Minjae Kim, and Ezra W. Zuckerman Sivan, "The Authentic Appeal of the Lying Demagogue: Proclaiming the Deeper Truth about Political Illegitimacy," *American Sociological Review*, vol. 83, no. 1 (2018), 1–33.

3 Henceforth, all parenthetical references are to Plato, *Republic*, ed. C. D. C. Reeve (Indianapolis: Hackett, 2004).

4 When putting aside Trump's character to examine his actions and policies, the thesis that Trump represents a tyrant weakens, see Walter R. Newell, "Introduction: Tyranny Two Years on," in *Tyrants: Power, Injustice, and Terror* (New York: Cambridge University Press, 2019), 1–30.

5 I do not claim to know Trump's soul. Rather, I claim that Trump's style reflects the disordered soul of Plato's tyrant. Hence, I claim that Trump has a "tyrant-like" style. See Angel Torres and Marc Sable who claim Trump has a tyrannical soul in "Leadership, Statesmanship and Tyranny: The Character and Rhetoric of Trump," in Angel Jaramillo Torres and Marc Benjamin (eds.), *Trump and Political Philosophy: Leadership, Statesmanship, and Tyranny* (Cham: Palgrave Macmillan, 2018), 1–14. For a full-length study of the nature of Plato's tyrant, see Cinzia Arruzza, *A Wolf in the City: Tyranny and the Tyrant in Plato's Republic* (New York: Oxford University Press, 2019).

6 Political theorists Lindsay Mahon Rathnam and Clifford Owrin echo these themes in their 2016 opinion piece, "Rob Ford and Donald Trump: Plato Would Get It." www.theglobeandmail.com/opinion/rob-ford-and-donald-trump-plato-would-get-it/article29425239/

7 For example, consider the outrage industry in "conservative" media that gave fuel to Trump's rise. See Jerry M. Berry and Sarah Sobieraj, *The Outrage Industry: Political Opinion Media and the New Incivility* (Oxford: Oxford University Press, 2016).
8 Arruza, *Wolf*, 63.
9 For examples of contemporary authors wrestling with these themes see Josiah Ober and Charles W. Hedrick, *Demokratia: A Conversation on Democracies, Ancient and Modern* (Princeton: Princeton University Press, 1996); and Valentina Arena, *Liberty: Ancient Ideas and Modern Perspectives* (New York: Routledge, 2021).
10 In this essay, I use "freedom" and "liberty" interchangeably. For an account of the differences and overlapping similarities between liberty and freedom, see David Hackett Fischer, introduction to *Liberty and Freedom: A Visual History of America's Founding Ideas* (New York: Oxford University Press, 2005), 1–16.
11 Federal Election Commission, *Federal Elections 2016: Election Results for the US President, the US Senate and the US House of Representatives*, December 2017, https://www.fec.gov/resources/cms-content/documents/federalelections2016.pdf.
12 Drew Desilver, "Biden's Victory Another Example of How Electoral College Wins Are Bigger Than Popular Vote Ones," Pew Research Center (website), December 11, 2020, https://www.pewresearch.org/fact-tank/2020/12/11/bidens-victory-another-example-of-how-electoral-college-wins-are-bigger-than-popular-vote-ones; Jacob Fabina, "Record High Turnout in 2020 General Election: Despite Pandemic Challenges, 2020 Election Had Largest Increase in Voting between Presidential Elections on Record," United States Census Bureau (website), April 29, 2021, https://www.census.gov/library/stories/2021/04/record-high-turnout-in-2020-general-election.html.
13 "Presidential Job Approval Center," Gallup (website), accessed October 12, 2021, https://news.gallup.com/interactives/185273/presidential-job-approval-center.aspx.
14 Philip Bump, "Trump Got the Most GOP Votes Ever—Both for and against Him—and Other Fun Facts," *Washington Post*, June 8, 2016, https://www.washingtonpost.com/news/the-fix/wp/2016/06/08/donald-trump-got-the-most-votes-in-gop-primary-history-a-historic-number-of-people-voted-against-him-too.
15 Natalie Colarossi, "Donald Trump's 73.6 Million Popular Votes Is over 7 Million More Than Any Sitting President in History," *Newsweek*, November 19, 2020, https://www.newsweek.com/donald-trumps-736-million-popular-votes-over-7-million-more-any-sitting-president-history-1548742.
16 Trump achieved that honor for the first time in his presidency. Zack Budryk writes that "the sitting U. S. president has been named [Gallup's] most-admired man in 60 out of 74 years, including all eight years of Obama's presidency and every year of George W. Bush's presidency except for 2008. Trump had finished second to Obama in 2017 and 2018." Prior to his presidency, Trump was in the top ten men from 1988 to 1990 and 2011. Zack Budryk, "Trump Ends Obama's 12-Year Run as Most Admired Man: Gallup," *The Hill*, December 29, 2020, https://thehill.com/homenews/administration/531906-trump-ends-obamas-12-year-run-as-most-admired-man-gallup.
17 For examples, see Jill Colvin and Aamer Madhani, "Policy vs. Personality: Undecideds Torn as Election Nears," AP News, October 18, 2020, https://apnews.com/article/election-2020-virus-outbreak-joe-biden-donald-trump-elections-894f413fca1f4e15b0754dcfa17fdd77.
18 Rachel Herz, *That's Disgusting: Unraveling the Mysteries of Repulsion* (New York: W. W. Norton, 2013), 294.
19 The reality, of course, might be quite different. Fear of humiliation, for example, seemed to have a role in guiding/restraining Trump's decision-making. Consider his

niece Mary Trump's characterization of Donald Trump as a "terrified little boy." Jane Mayer, "Why Trump Can't Afford to Lose," *New Yorker*, November 1, 2020, https://www.newyorker.com/magazine/2020/11/09/why-trump-cant-afford-to-lose.

20 For an explanation of why a lack of forms resonates with democratic citizens, see Harvey Mansfield, "The Forms and Formalities of Liberty," *Public Interest*, vol. 70 (1983), 121–31.

21 Charles Taylor, *A Secular Age* (Cambridge: Harvard University Press, 2009).

22 Jerome B. Schneewind, *The Invention of Autonomy: A History of Modern Moral Philosophy* (Cambridge: Cambridge University Press, 1998). See also Brent Edwin Cusher and Mark A. Menaldo, *Leadership and the Unmasking of Authenticity: The Philosophy of Self-Knowledge and Deception* (Cheltenham: Edward Elgar, 2018).

23 "Authenticity" is a contested term historically and presently. I put forward the uncontroversial claim that there is a relationship among freedom, individual autonomy, and authenticity. I do not mean to suggest that authenticity can be reduced to "doing as one pleases" or "being yourself." That simplistic conception is, however, an attractive understanding of authenticity, as I claim in what follows.

24 Ben Zimmer, "'Authenticity' in the 2016 Campaign," *Wall Street Journal*, September 18, 2015, https://www.wsj.com/articles/authenticity-in-the-2016-campaign-1442591796; Tommy Shane, "The Semiotics of Authenticity: Indexicality in Donald Trump's Tweets," *Social Media and Society*, vol. 4, no. 3 (2018), https://doi.org/10.1177/2056305118800315; Greg Sargent, "Who Is the 'Authenticity' Candidate of 2016? Yup: It's Donald Trump," *Washington Post*, December 11, 2015, https://www.washingtonpost.com/blogs/plum-line/wp/2015/12/11/who-is-the-authenticity-candidate-of-2016-yup-its-donald-trump.

25 See Erica J. Seifert, *The Politics of Authenticity in Presidential Campaigns, 1976–2008* (Jefferson, NC: McFarland, 2012).

26 Noah Johnson, "Ivanka Trump Discusses President's Accomplishments during Wilmington Visit," Wilmington StarNews Online, September 14 2020, https://www.starnewsonline.com/story/special/2020/09/14/ivanka-trump-discusses-presidentrsquos-accomplishments-during-wilmington-visit/114019260.

27 For one example in the popular press of this view see Michael Gerson, "Trump's 'Authenticity' Is Merely Moral Laziness and Cruelty," *Washington Post*, January 7, 2019, https://www.washingtonpost.com/opinions/trumps-authenticity-is-merely-moral-laziness-and-cruelty/2019/01/07/b01f098a-12a9-11e9-b6ad-9cfd62dbb0a8_story.html.

28 Katya Kupelian, "Barbara Corcoran on Donald Trump: 'He Is the Best Salesman I've Ever Met in My Life'," Business Insider, December 18, 2018, https://www.businessinsider.com/trump-best-salesman-barbara-corcoran-has-ever-met-2018-12.

29 Michael Kruse, "The Power of Trump's Positive Thinking," *Politico Magazine* (website), October 13, 2017, https://www.politico.com/magazine/story/2017/10/13/donald-trump-positive-thinking-215704.

30 See Ronald Beiner, "The Soul of the Tyrant, and the Souls of You and Me: Plato's Understanding of Tyranny," in Toivo Koivukoski and David Edward Tabachnick (eds.), *Confronting Tyranny: Ancient Lessons for Global Politics* (Lanham: Roman and Littlefield, 2019), 181–96. See also Arruzza, *Wolf in the City*.

31 For an overview of the concept of freedom in ancient Greece, see Kurt A. Raaflaub, *The Discovery of Freedom in Ancient Greece* (Chicago: University of Chicago Press, 2004).

32 Hannah Miet, "40 Ounces of Freedom: Big Soda Fights Bloomberg's Ban," *Atlantic*, July 1, 2012, https://www.theatlantic.com/national/archive/2012/07/40-ounces-freedom-big-soda-fights-bloombergs-ban/326392. Corporate interests benefiting from the sale

of sugary drinks were all too happy to go along with the narrative of "threatened freedom" to protect their profits.

33 It is worth noting that antimaskers were a sizable group during the 1918 pandemic in the United States. See Christine Hauser, "The Mask Slackers of 1918," *New York Times*, August 3, 2020, updated December 10, 2020, https://www.nytimes.com/2020/08/03/us/mask-protests-1918.html.

34 Grant Schulte and Amy Forliti, "Nurses Wanted: Swamped Hospitals Scramble for Pandemic Help," AP News, December 2, 2020, https://apnews.com/article/nurses-wanted-swamped-hospitals-pandemic-0509a4a0b9e9860ad6be60379bc20a41.

35 Sigmund Freud, "On Narcissism," in *The Complete Psychological Works of Sigmund Freud, vol. 14, On the History of the Psycho-Analytic Movement: Papers on Metapsychology and Other Works* (London: Vintage, 2001), 91.

36 A human being, as Aristotle puts it in the *Politics*, is the worst of animals when "separated from law and justice" (1253a33).

37 Seth Benardete, *Socrates' Second Sailing; On Plato's Republic* (Chicago: University of Chicago Press, 1989), 201.

38 "Dreaming is a large part of democratic possibility, and when dreaming has become fully realized, it has become tyranny." Benardete, 199. Consider, Michael Flynn, the former national security adviser pardoned by Trump, dreamy statement when speaking from the stage at a Trump rally. "That's pretty cool. Imagine just being able to jump in a helicopter and just go for a joy ride around Washington." Ashraf Kahlil, "Tempers flare as Trump supporters rally in Washington" AP News, December 12, 2020, https://apnews.com/article/election-2020-donald-trump-politics-elections-8a505d0ae0915e0c9297208a76d7838a

39 Newell, "Introduction," 7.

40 Aakash Singh Rathore, *Plato's Labyrinth: Sophistries, Lies and Conspiracies in Socratic Dialogues* (United Kingdom: Taylor & Francis, 2017), 95. See also Roger Boesche, *Theories of Tyranny: From Plato to Arendt* (University Park, PA: Pennsylvania State University Press, 1996), 46.

41 Philip Rucker, Josh Dawsey, Shane Harris, and Ashley Parker, "Aides Weigh Resignations, Removal Options as Trump Rages against Perceived Betrayals," *Washington Post*, January 7, 2021, https://www.washingtonpost.com/politics/trump-resignations-25th-amendment/2021/01/07/e131ce10-50a3-11eb-bda4-615aaefd0555_story.html.

42 Ashley Parker, Josh Dawsey, and Philip Rucker, "Six Hours of Paralysis: Inside Trump's Failure to Act after a Mob Stormed the Capitol," *Washington Post*, January 11, 2021, https://www.washingtonpost.com/politics/trump-mob-failure/2021/01/11/36a46e2e-542e-11eb-a817-e5e7f8a406d6_story.html; Richard Cowan and Sarah N. Lynch, "Police Recount Mayhem and 'Attempted Coup' in US Capitol Riot,"Reuters, July 27, 2021, https://www.reuters.com/world/us/police-who-defended-us-capitol-testify-riot-probes-first-hearing-2021-07-27.

43 "Video Shows Capitol 'Mob Calling for the Death of the Vice President,' Plaskett Says," PBS Newshour (website), February 10, 2021, https://www.pbs.org/newshour/politics/watch-video-shows-capitol-mob-calling-for-the-death-of-the-vice-president-plaskett-says; Elaine Godfrey, "It Was Supposed to Be So Much Worse," *Atlantic*, January 9, 2021, https://www.theatlantic.com/politics/archive/2021/01/trump-rioters-wanted-more-violence-worse/617614.

44 For a timeline of events, see "Capitol Riots Timeline: The Evidence Presented against Trump," BBC News, February 13, 2021, https://www.bbc.com/news/world-us-canada-56004916. Since the events on January 6, allies of former President Trump have tried

to refocus and reframe the narrative of what happened on that day. See Lisa Mascaro, "Capitol Rally Seeks to Rewrite Jan. 6 by Exalting Rioters," AP News, September 13, 2021, https://apnews.com/article/joe-biden-donald-trump-capitol-siege-d2fb23af3f01387412a1a00b4eac531c.

45 Ross Douthat, "Donald Trump Doesn't Want Power," *New York Times*, May 19, 2020, https://www.nytimes.com/2020/05/19/opinion/coronavirus-trump-orban.html.

46 Michael Kruse and Noah Weiland, "Donald Trump's Greatest Self-Contradictions," *Politico Magazine* (website), May 5, 2016, https://www.politico.com/magazine/story/2016/05/donald-trump-2016-contradictions-213869.

47 For a view of Trump's attitude toward truth-telling as that of the tyrant, see Patrick Lee Miller, "Truth, Trump, Tyranny: Plato and the Sophists in an Era of 'Alternative Facts'," in Angel Jaramillo Torres and Marc Benjamin Sable (eds.), *Trump and Political Philosophy: Leadership, Statesmanship, and Tyranny* (Cham: Palgrave Macmillan, 2018), 17–32.

48 Jill Filipovic, "Trump Is Consistent: There's No Issue He Won't Take Both Sides On," *Washington Post*, October 29, 2020, https://www.washingtonpost.com/outlook/trump-meadows-cnn-flip-flop-obamacare/2020/10/29/7becb978-1969-11eb-82db-60b15c874105_story.html.

49 Robert O. Paxton, "I've Hesitated to Call Donald Trump a Fascist. Until Now," *Newsweek*, January 11, 2021, https://www.newsweek.com/robert-paxton-trump-fascist-1560652. See also Federico Finchelstein, "Donald Trump Has Blurred the Line between Populism and Fascism in a Dangerous Way," *Washington Post*, July 9, 2021, https://www.washingtonpost.com/outlook/2021/07/09/donald-trump-has-blurred-line-between-populism-fascism-dangerous-way.

50 We should refrain from focusing on the Trump phenomenon as fascist, as such a focus distracts from the historical peculiarities surrounding Trump's rise in the United States. It also feeds into the "reckless expansion" of the terms socialism and fascism, which the Left and Right overuse against their opponents. See Timothy W. Luke, "January 6, 2021: Another Day That Will Live in Infamy?," *Telos: Critical Theory of the Contemporary 194* (Spring, 2021), 153–54; Christopher Lasch, *The True and Only Heaven; Progress and Its Critics* (New York: W.W. Norton & Company, 1991), 25.

51 Nick Penzenstadler, Steve Reilly, David Wilson, Karen Yi, Pim Linders, John Kelly, and Jeff Dionise, "Donald Trump Three Decades, 4,095 Lawsuits," USA Today, accessed on October 17, 2021, https://www.usatoday.com/pages/interactives/trump-lawsuits.

52 Michael Kruse, "The Fear behind Donald Trump's Obsession with Immunity," *Politico Magazine* (website), October 22, 2020, https://www.politico.com/news/magazine/2020/10/22/fear-donald-trump-obsession-immunity-430928.

53 James D. Zirin, "Trump's Last Gasp," *The Hill*, December 13, 2020, https://thehill.com/opinion/judiciary/529965-trumps-last-gasp. "Cohn taught Trump all the dirty tricks of the trade. Always claim you won when you lost. If you do lose, change the rules," writes Zirin, former federal prosecutor and author of *Plaintiff in Chief: A Portrait of Donald Trump in 3500 Lawsuits*.

54 Michael Kruse, "The Final Lesson Donald Trump Never Learned from Roy Cohn," *Politico Magazine* (website), September 19, 2019, https://www.politico.com/magazine/story/2019/09/19/roy-cohn-donald-trump-documentary-228144.

55 Kruse, "Fear."

56 Kruse, "Final Lesson."

57 I do not mean to suggest that everyone who feels powerless will find the tyrant appealing. Other segments of the powerless might feel hopeless and therefore not find the tyrant or any leader appealing; then again, others might place their hope in other political leaders

and/or movements. As for Trump's supporters, it is important to recognize their diverse socio-economic, geographic, and educational backgrounds. See Robert A. Pape and Keven Ruby, "The Capitol Rioters Aren't Like Other Extremists," *Atlantic*, February 2, 2021, https://www.theatlantic.com/ideas/archive/2021/02/the-capitol-rioters-arent-like-other-extremists/617895; "Top Contributors, Federal Election Data for Donald Trump, 2020 Cycle," Open Secrets (website), accessed on October 17, 2021, https://www.opensecrets.org/2020-presidential-race/donald-trump/contributors?id=N00023864; Laura K. Field, "The Highbrow Conspiracism of the New Intellectual Right A Sampling from the Trump Years," Niskanen Center (website), April 19, 2021, https://www.niskanencenter.org/the-highbrow-conspiracism-of-the-new-intellectual-right-a-sampling-from-the-trump-years.

58 The reaction to a threat of a loss of power is arguably at the heart of conservatism. Corey Robin describes conservatism as "the felt experience of having power, seeing it threatened, and trying to win it back." Corey Robin, *The Reactionary Mind: Conservatism from Edmund Burke to Donald Trump* (New York: Oxford University Press, 2018), 4.

59 For one example of an analysis of the rage of the "left-behind" who found Trump appealing, see Susan McWilliams, "This Political Theorist Predicted the Rise of Trumpism. His Name Was Hunter S. Thompson," *Nation*, December 16, 2018, https://www.thenation.com/article/archive/this-political-theorist-predicted-the-rise-of-trumpism-his-name-was-hunter-s-thompson.

60 Publius Decius Mus, "The Flight 93 Election," *Claremont Review of Books* digital exclusive, September 5, 2016, https://claremontreviewofbooks.com/digital/the-flight-93-election.

61 Even after "the spirit of lawlessness [that was] unleashed" on January 6th, Charles Kesler insisted that courage is the element of Trump's "political manner" that should be adopted by the "movement he has led. . . The courage he shows in confronting political correctness, cancel culture, and the scorn of progressive censors. His successors cannot afford to lose his wonderful effrontery in opposing, for example, the continuing ideological purges of American history and heroes." Charles R. Kesler, "After January 6th: The Future of Trump and Trumpism," *Claremont Review of Books* (Winter, 2021), https://claremontreviewofbooks.com/after-january-6th.

62 Consider the wealthy individuals attracted to his regulatory rollbacks and tax cuts. See Michela Tindera, "Here Are the Billionaires Backing Donald Trump's Campaign," *Forbes* (website), April 17, 2020, https://www.forbes.com/sites/michelatindera/2020/04/17/here-are-the-billionaires-backing-donald-trumps-campaign-as-of-february-2020; and "Top Contributors."

63 Trump may have cared about being popular and liked, but that form of caring is purely self-referential in nature; it loses sight of the other for the sake of the self.

64 Edward-Isaac Dovere, "Trump Struggles with Consoler-in-Chief Role," Politico (website), February 16, 2018, https://www.politico.eu/article/donald-trump-struggles-with-consoler-in-chief-role.

65 After being deemed well enough from his struggle with Covid-19 to be released from Walter Reed, Trump planned to "wear a Superman T-shirt, which he would reveal as a symbol of strength when he ripped open the top layer. He ultimately did not go ahead with the stunt."; Annie Karni and Maggie Haberman, "Trump Makes First Appearance since Leaving Walter Reed," *New York Times*, October 10, 2020, updated October 12, 2020, https://www.nytimes.com/2020/10/10/us/politics/trump-white-house-coronavirus.html. See the chapter "Reach Out and Elect Someone" in Neil Postman, *Amusing Ourselves to Death: Public Discourse in the Age of Show Business* (New York: Viking Penguin, 1985).

66 These thoughts on outrageousness are informed by Deborah C. Stewart, Lisa Marchiano, and Joseph R. Lee, "Outrageous!: What Drives Shocking Behaviors," February 27, 2020, in *This Jungian Life,* podcast, MP3 audio, 61:03, https://thisjungianlife.com/episode-100-outrageous-what-drives-shocking-behaviors.

67 Wilson Carey McWilliams, "Liberty, Equality, and the Problem of Community," in Patrick J. Deneen and Susan J. McWilliams (eds.), *The Democratic Soul: A Wilson Carey McWilliams Reader* (Lexington: University of Kentucky Press, 2011), 21–43.

68 McWilliams, "Liberty," 39.

69 McWilliams, "Liberty," 22.

70 For an account of how an undemocratic conception of freedom came to prominence in contemporary democracies see Annelien De Dijn, *Freedom: An Unruly History* (Cambridge, MA: Harvard University Press, 2020).

71 That fragility was on full display in the attack on the Capitol, not to mention in the countless coup attempts endured by democracies around the world.

72 Consider the policies put forward in the journal *American Affairs*, a quarterly journal of public policy and political thought that originated in solidarity with what Trump represented for conservatism in the United States. Julius Krein, the founder of the journal, eventually denounced Trump after his response to the Unite the Right rally at Charlottesville in 2017 but continued facilitating a forum in which the meaning and future of conservatism could be explored. See "About *American Affairs*," *American Affairs* (website), accessed October 18, 2021, https://americanaffairsjournal.org/about.

73 Those on the Left and the Right in the United States fear that the other side harbors such ambitions. Consider former US Attorney General William Barr's description of the Left: "They're not interested in compromise, they're not interested in dialectic exchange of views. They're interested in total victory." Nathan Lane, "US Attorney General Barr Says the Left Wants to Tear Down the System," Reuters, August 9, 2020, https://www.reuters.com/article/usa-congress-barr-idINKCN256053.

74 "Text: Vice President Gore Concedes Election," *Washington Post*, December 13, 2000, https://www.washingtonpost.com/wp-srv/onpolitics/elections/goretext121300.htm.

75 Michael R. Blood and Jill Colvin, "Pence 'Proud' of His Role Certifying 2020 Presidential Election Results," AP News, June 25, 2021, https://apnews.com/article/joe-biden-michael-pence-constitutions-government-and-politics-a8e29ab2c6bc5a5f-ecd9e4236eb8f3c3.

76 Clinton, upon being defeated by Trump in the 2016 presidential race, followed Gore's lead by speedily conceding. Later on, however, she would claim that Trump knew he was an "illegitimate president. . . . Former president Jimmy Carter used similar language" when describing Trump's presidency. Colby Itkowitz, "Hillary Clinton: Trump Is an 'Illegitimate President'," *Washington Post*, September 6, 2019, https://www.washingtonpost.com/politics/hillary-clinton-trump-is-an-illegitimate-president/2019/09/26/29195d5a-e099-11e9-b199-f638bf2c340f_story.html.

77 Luciani Floridi, ed., *The Onlife Manifesto: Being Human in a Hyperconnected Era* (Cham: Springer International, 2015).

78 Dale Beran, *It Came from Something Awful: How a Toxic Troll Army Accidentally Memed Donald Trump into Office* (New York: All Points, 2019); Alfonso Vergaray, "Anonymous (2004–present)," in Scott Ainsworth and Brian Harward (eds.), *Political Parties, Interest Groups, and Organizations that Shaped America: An Encyclopedia and Document Collection*, vol. 1 (Santa Barbara, CA: ABC-CLIO, 2019).

79 C. Thi Nguyen, "Escape the Echo Chamber," *Aeon* (website), April 9, 2018, https://aeon.co/essays/why-its-as-hard-to-escape-an-echo-chamber-as-it-is-to-flee-a-cult.

80 The challenge of feeling like one is part of a large and plural nation has been an enduring puzzle in the United States, requiring different considerations by different citizens at different times. See James Baldwin, "The Discovery of What It Means to Be an American," in *The Price of the Ticket: Collected Nonfiction, 1948–1985* (Boston: Beacon, 2021), 179–84; Samuel Goldman, *After Nationalism: Being American in an Age of Division* (College Park, PA: Pennsylvania State University Press, 2021); and Mehnaaz Momen, *The Paradox of Citizenship in American Politics: Ideals and Reality* (Cham: Springer International, 2017).

81 See Paul W. Ludwig, *Rediscovering Political Friendship: Aristotle's Theory and Modern Identity, Community, and Equality* (Cambridge: Cambridge University Press, 2020).

82 McWilliams, "Liberty," 39.

5

POLITICS AS THEATER

Trump and Machiavelli's Political Actors

Michael Harvey

On January 6, 2021, two months after President Donald J. Trump lost his bid for reelection, a rally, known variously as the "Stop the Steal" rally, or the "March to Save America," or the "March for Trump," brought tens of thousands of Trump supporters to Washington, DC. They came, by and large, because they believed Trump's claims—amplified endlessly in conservative media—that the election had been stolen from him, and that the president-elect, Joe Biden, was illegitimate. "The cavalry is coming, Mr. President!," read one December tweet from a January 6 organizer (still, at time of writing, proudly pinned to the author's Twitter account). They came, by the thousands, to rally and protest—and, ultimately, to violently invade the US Capitol—in an attempt to block Congress's certification of the November results, which was scheduled for that day.

The events of that day can be understood in many ways, from defense of democracy, to a protest that got out of hand, to insurrection. But Donald Trump's speech at noon on January 6, in which he called on his supporters to march to the Capitol to demand that, for the first time in American history, the results of a presidential election that had been tallied and reported by the states, and certified by the Electoral College, be rejected by Congress—this speech is best understood as a signal moment of political theater.

Event Strategies, a company that had helped manage events for both of Trump's presidential campaigns, set up a stage on the south side of the White House, facing the Washington Monument, from which President Trump and his entourage could watch, and address the crowd. At noon on January 6, after other speakers had preceded him, President Trump gave an hour-long speech. He began, as so often, by asserting a Manichean clash: his defense of the truth against his opponents' lies. He claimed that "hundreds of thousands" of

DOI: 10.4324/9781003110361-5

supporters were present, and that if lower attendance figures were reported, it would be due to malice from a hostile media:

> Media will not show the magnitude of this crowd. Even I, when I turned on today, I looked, and I saw thousands of people here. But you don't see hundreds of thousands of people behind you because they don't want to show that.
>
> We have hundreds of thousands of people here and I just want them to be recognized by the fake news media. Turn your cameras please and show what's really happening out here because these people are not going to take it any longer. They're not going to take it any longer. Go ahead. Turn your cameras, please. Would you show? They came from all over the world, actually, but they came from all over our country.
>
> I just really want to see what they do. I just want to see how they covered. I've never seen anything like it. But it would be really great if we could be covered fairly by the media. The media is the biggest problem we have as far as I'm concerned, single biggest problem.

Throughout his populist political career, Trump has often relied on this polarization of America's political conflict—"patriots" versus "enemy of the people," truth versus lies. In the January 6 speech, he cast himself as a simple, plain-speaking defender of truth:

> I'm honest. And I just, again, I want to thank you. It's just a great honor to have this kind of crowd and to be before you and hundreds of thousands of American patriots who are committed to the honesty of our elections and the integrity of our glorious republic.

By contrast, not only his political opponents but even America's media also were utterly corrupt and dishonest:

> We don't have a free and fair press. Our media is not free, it's not fair. It suppresses thought, it suppresses speech and it's become the enemy of the people. It's become the enemy of the people. It's the biggest problem we have in this country.

After praising his administration's achievements in his typically superlative but vague phrasing ("We've created the greatest economy in history. We rebuilt our military. We get you the biggest tax cuts in history. Right? We got you the biggest regulation cuts."),[1] Trump laid out, in a series of false but vivid claims, his case for how the election had been stolen—for instance, that in Pennsylvania, more absentee ballots had been counted than were mailed out, or that in Wisconsin, "corrupt Democrat-run cities deployed more than 500 illegal, unmanned, unsecured drop boxes, which collected a minimum of 91,000 unlawful votes."

And, eventually, like any good political speech, he included a call to action:

> Now, it is up to Congress to confront this egregious assault on our democracy. And after this, we're going to walk down, and I'll be there with you, we're going to walk down, we're going to walk down.
>
> Anyone you want, but I think right here, we're going to walk down to the Capitol, and we're going to cheer on our brave senators and congressmen and women, and we're probably not going to be cheering so much for some of them.
>
> Because you'll never take back our country with weakness. You have to show strength and you have to be strong. We have come to demand that Congress do the right thing and only count the electors who have been lawfully slated, lawfully slated.
>
> I know that everyone here will soon be marching over to the Capitol building to peacefully and patriotically make your voices heard.

"I'll be there with you . . . we're going to walk down to the Capitol." And then, at the end of the speech, when the crowd started moving toward the Capitol, Trump turned around, exited the stage, and went back inside the White House. The performance was over. Back to watching TV to hear the reviews.

★ ★ ★

All politics is, in some core sense, theatrical. The necessity to persuade, the interweaving of authentic identity and assumed role, of sincere belief and enacted pretense, is embedded in every political system, whatever its basis for power, authority, and representation. Persuasion is never merely rational or procedural—it is always partly theatrical, even if the persuasion is needed merely to affirm what has already been decided.

Five centuries ago Niccolò Machiavelli analyzed the theatrics of politics more extensively and imaginatively than any previous thinker. Not only in *The Prince* but also in works like *The History of Florence*, and indeed in his plays, the image of politics as a theater becomes the central metaphor for—actually, more than metaphor, a literal descriptor of—politics. And the corollary of this view is that playing to the audience is a critical political task of any would-be political actor—and that audience is dumb. Many, Machiavelli says, see the large strokes, not the fine details, the careful preparation, or the hidden motives:

> Men in general judge more by their eyes than by their hands, because seeing is given to everyone, touching to a few. Everyone sees how you appear, few touch what you are. . . . For the vulgar are taken in by the

appearance and the outcome of a thing, and in the world there is no one but the vulgar.[2]

The right understanding of theatricality is thus, for Machiavelli, an essential part of the art of the ruler. Machiavelli says in *The Prince* that a ruler "should at suitable times of the year keep the people occupied with festivals and spectacles." One of the political actors treated in *The Prince*, Ferdinand of Aragon, "has always done and ordered great things, which have always kept the minds of his subjects in suspense and admiration, and occupied with their outcome." The emperor Severus possessed such *virtù*, Machiavelli says in the same work, that even though the people were oppressed by him, "he was always ably to rule prosperously because his *virtù* made him so admirable" that the people "remained somehow astonished and stupefied."[3]

A ruler's ability to act theatrically is closely related to their ability to deceive. Machiavelli's most extreme and even comical evocation of a skilled deceiver concerns a man performing on the very highest, most widely viewed stage. Of Pope Alexander VI (Alexander Borgia), he declares,

> Alexander VI never did anything, nor ever thought of anything, but how to deceive men. . . . And there never was a man with greater efficacy in asserting a thing, and in affirming it with greater oaths, who observed it less; nonetheless, his deceits succeeded at his will, because he well knew this aspect of the world.[4]

Like the "cunning, astute" *frati* of Machiavelli's comedy, *Mandragola*, Pope Alexander is well versed in public deceptions, in playing a role for a rapt and trusting audience. By noting Pope Alexander's ability to affirm lies with the highest oaths, Machiavelli suggests that the most solemn ceremonies of the church are the most highly developed instances of theater and deceit in his world, and that if one is to attain the supreme position of Pope, it has nothing to do with piety and everything to do with the single-minded ability to play a role.

Perhaps the best-known instance of Machiavelli's theatrical treatment of the art of ruling is the story of how Alexander's son, Cesare Borgia, made use of Remirro de Orco. Borgia sought to pacify the citizens of the province of Romagna by relying on the harsh governorship of Remirro, "a cruel and ready man." Remirro was so brutally successful that Borgia soon came to fear either that he would lose Romagna to Remirro or that the people would rise up against him. So having gotten the use out of Remirro that he needed, Borgia decided not merely to get rid of him but also to do it in a fashion that would captivate the people and stamp Borgia as the new actor on their stage to be watched. Machiavelli describes his act as an electric bit of theater: "one morning at Cesena he had Messer Remirro laid in two pieces in the public square with a block of wood and a bloody sword near him." The scene, with its carefully chosen props, turned the people into an audience "satisfied and stupefied" by the "ferocity of this spectacle."[5] One of the reasons Machiavelli praised Borgia so highly was Borgia's appreciation of the theatricality of political action, and the powerful effect of the right act well performed at the right moment. Cesare Borgia, one suspects, would not have gone back inside the White House at the end of his speech.

★ ★ ★

One of the most striking instances of Machiavelli's theatrical treatment of power—and perhaps his best approximation to the meteoric virtuosity, the fall as well as the rise, of Donald Trump's political theater—is found in his account of the short, turbulent career of Walter, the 14th-century tyrant of Florence. Walter ruled Florence for just ten months, from 1342 to 1343. He first arrived on the scene, Machiavelli relates, long before, in 1326, after the Florentines, defeated in battle by Castruccio Castracani of Lucca, turned to the King of Naples and his son, the Duke of Calabria, for aid. The Duke sent Walter to be his deputy in Florence. Machiavelli describes Walter's initial appearance as, in effect, a disguise: "his conduct was so modest and so contrary to his nature that everybody loved him."[6] Fifteen years went by before Walter reappeared. He did so once again during a time of Florentine turmoil involving Lucca, which had just been lost to Pisa. Once again, the Florentines appealed for aid to the King of Naples; once again, Walter was sent to rule as deputy. In Florence, popular resentment at the nobles who had lost Lucca was widespread, and many of the nobles wanted a strong man to rise up and chastise the people. Behind the scenes, some of the nobles urged Walter to take power, and he was quick to try. In order "to give himself a reputation" for severity and justice, he punished those nobles who had been associated with the failed campaign against Lucca. These measures worked. Machiavelli describes the effect as someone watching a performance: "As the Duke passed through the streets, loud voices praised his gallant spirit. . . . [E]verybody, to show that he was his friend, had the Duke's insignia painted on his house."[7]

The whole story of the Duke is told with this attention to performance and appearance. Machiavelli says that "to give himself a greater appearance of religion and of kindness," the Duke chose to live in a convent. When he decided he was ready to seize power, he gathered the people before the convent like an audience in a theater: "he had it announced by criers that on the following morning all the people should assemble in the piazza of Santa Croce, in his presence."[8] The next day, the ceremony unfolded as a piece of theater. At first, it proceeded according to a script agreed to by Walter and the Florentine nobles: "the agreements made between the Signoria and him were read to the people." But, at this point, Walter's deft theatrical management changed the script which the nobles thought they had arranged. The Florentine nobles had agreed to grant him sovereignty for one year, but when the ceremony reached this provision, Machiavelli relates that some in the audience, in a disruption arranged by Walter by means of a timely bribe, broke in: "And when they came, in the course of reading, to that part where for one year he had obtained sovereignty, there was a shout among the people: 'For life!'" One of the nobles rose in order to regain control of the stage, but he was shouted down. At the end of the ceremony, Walter entered the Palace, tore up the people's banner, and raised his own ensigns. The duped Signors, "bewildered and dishonored," exit the scene.[9]

Now the acknowledged ruler of Florence, Walter tried to hold onto power by enticing the people with spectacle and theater:

> he established for the lower class and the humble people more companies, to which, honoring them with splendid titles, he gave banners and money, so that one part of them went through the city in festive array and the other with great pomp received those who were celebrating.[10]

Walter literally turned the streets of Florence into a theater and the people into both audience and actors.

But gradually the people began to see past Walter's performance and to hate what they saw. In keeping with his treatment of Walter, Machiavelli represents the growing disillusion in visual terms:

> they saw the majesty of their state ruined. . . . Those accustomed not to see any regal splendor could not but feel pain whenever they encountered that ruler, surrounded with armed retainers on foot and on horseback. . . . seeing their shame near at hand, they were forced to honor him. . . . they saw the frequent executions and incessant taxes.

The Archbishop of Florence, who in his own public performances, his sermons, had once praised the Duke, now began to rue his own role in events: "when he saw the Duke in power and realized his tyrannical ways, he knew that he had deceived his own city." When Walter punished a man who had complained about taxes, he acts as if to silence a rival actor, having the man's tongue cut out. Machiavelli dramatizes Walter's tyrannical spirit by suggesting it is a consuming desire to be the only actor on a stage. Walter at last reduces the whole city to his captive audience: Florence, "accustomed to doing and speaking of everything . . ., could not endure to have her hands bound and her mouth tight shut."[11]

Yet, although Machiavelli strongly criticizes Walter's theatrical instinct as an expression of a tyrannical spirit, it is really, as he tells it, Walter's failure to be theatrical enough that causes his fall from power. Machiavelli conveys this with a reference to Walter's failure in the paradigmatic action of the political actor, the public appearance on horseback to assert his power. The Duke, who had come to be hated by the nobles and the people, escaped one assassination attempt. When he learned that there was a conspiracy against him, he was urged to act strongly, in the manner of Liverotto or Michele di Lando (see below) at their moments of crisis: "Messer Francesco Brunelleschi and Messer Uguccione Buondelmonti advised the Duke to ride armed through the city and to put to death those he arrested." But the Duke, afraid that his enemies were too many and his forces too few, declined to play this role. Instead, he made another plan, to summon three hundred leading citizens to the palace and kill or arrest them. Before he can carry this out, however, they react as he dared not: they are "given courage to take arms and plan to die like men with arms in their hands, rather than like cattle to be led to the slaughterhouse."[12]

After the uprising scattered Walter's forces, he made one last effort to recover his position through performance.

> The Duke . . . attempted to gain the people over by various kind acts; having the prisoners come before him, with loving and gracious words he freed them; Antonio Adimari, though to that man's displeasure, he made a knight. He had his ensigns removed from over the palace and those of the people put there.

But Walter is out of sync, at the end, with the script. His words and actions are dismissed by Machiavelli as "things which, done late and at the wrong time, because they were forced and without generosity, helped him little."[13]

It is extraordinary to what degree Machiavelli tells Walter's story in terms of performance and show. And yet, through all this, he has not described his appearance. When he finally does so at the very end of the story, the description carries dramatic and even moral power, as if in the end Walter's appearance explained everything about him: "Nor was his appearance less hateful in nature than were his manners, for he was little and dark, his beard was long and thin, so that in every way he deserved to be hated."[14] It is the final dismissal of Walter the actor to reduce him to an obvious stage-villain.

Yet had the Duke acted with greater wisdom, Machiavelli would surely have found less occasion to condemn him as a tyrant and might have likened him to one of his heroes, Castruccio Castracani of Lucca. Machiavelli intends the careful reader to contrast the Duke's weakness with Castruccio's strength, for the Duke's initial appearance in Florence is occasioned by Castruccio's defeat of the Florentine mercenary army, and his reappearance fifteen years later is also caused by a Florentine military defeat involving Lucca. There is no substantive moral difference between the two men, who both practiced numerous frauds; the only real difference is that Castruccio was able to direct his energies into making Lucca a strong and aggressive state, while the Duke occupied himself in domestic turmoils, preventing one conspiracy after another and planning one performance after another.

Another master of theater in Machiavelli's writings is Michele di Lando. Michele was a humble woolcomber who, as Machiavelli tells it in the *History of Florence*, rose out of obscurity during the Ciompi rebellion of 1378 to preserve good government in Florence. The Ciompi rebellion unleashed a brief and ferocious civil war in Florence, pitting poor against rich. The rebellion sent thousands rampaging through the streets. After a while, the mob focused its energies and seized the palace of the Podestà, Florence's ruler. As the mob entered the palace, Michele seized control of events. Machiavelli tells the story as a perfect bit of theater, down to Michele's prop, costume and stage management:

> When the men of the lower class entered the Palace, Michele di Lando, a woolcomber, had the standard of the Gonfalonier of Justice in his hand. This man, barefoot and wearing little clothing, with all the crowd behind him, went up the stairs, and when he was in the audience chamber of the Signors he stopped and, turning to the crowd, said: "Look; this Palace is yours and this city is in your hands. What do you think we should do now?" They all answered that they wanted him to be Gonfalonier and Signor, and to rule them and the city as he wished.[15]

Michele transformed the mob into a docile audience, whom he prompted to make him their master. A "sagacious and prudent man," he felt a duty to restore order and transform mob rule into the rule of law. To that end, he relied on another theatrical device: "to frighten everyone he set up a gallows in the Public Square." Machiavelli concludes his discussion of the Ciompi rebellion by praising Michele very highly:

> In courage, in prudence and in goodness he surpassed every citizen of his time. . . . His prudence enabled him to manage affairs in such a way that many of his party yielded to him; the others he overcame with arms.[16]

Michele's performance is a perfect Machiavellian union of strength and appearance.

Machiavelli may intend the reader to contrast Walter's failure to use theatricality with Michele di Lando's parallel success. Walter rose up and was cast down in the space of ten months, we are told. A generation later Michele rose up to power and, like Walter, within a year, was faced with a revolt against his rule. Machiavelli, when he describes Michele's bold decision to mount a horse and face his enemies, alludes back to Walter's failure:

> "Michele," he says, "determined to act beforehand, thinking that it would be more glorious for him to make an attack than to wait for his enemy

> within walls and, like his predecessors, to have to run away with dishonor to the Palace and shame to himself."

When Machiavelli passes judgment on Michele, he makes the comparison with Walter explicit: "If his spirit had been either wicked or ambitious, the republic would have entirely lost her liberty and would have come under a tyranny more severe than that of the Duke of Athens."[17] It is a retrospective denunciation of Walter's failure of nerve. Few other characters in Machiavelli's writings are depicted so patently as performers; it is the irony of Walter's performance that he fails not because he is an actor playing a role but because he fails to embrace the role deeply enough.

One lesson one should take from a comparison of these two 14th-century Florentine strong men, Walter and Michele di Lando, is that the better one's grasp of the theatrics of power, the better one can play the role of ruler. But one should realize that for Machiavelli there are limits to what theatricality can achieve. He is not a simple enthusiast of performance and spectacle and makes some strong criticisms of the theatrical impulse. Theatricality by itself is an inadequate vehicle to political power. Machiavelli's strongest criticism of excessive reliance on theater also appears in the *History of Florence*, in his treatment of the city's 15th-century rulers, the Medici.

At first appearance, it seems that the Medici are exemplary Machiavellian performers. In all of his work, they are the rulers most persistently associated with theater. Piero, the son of Cosimo, the great founder of the Medici regime, and Piero's own son, Lorenzo, excelled in spectacles and relied on them as a crucial political resource to keep order within the state. A year after the death of Cosimo, the less-talented Piero resorted to spectacles to "quiet" the people and "remove their thoughts from the government." One of these shows was a representation of the journey of the three kings from the East—"so elaborate and splendid that the entire city was kept busy for many months in preparing and presenting it."[18]

Machiavelli associates such shows most closely with Piero's son, Lorenzo, who ruled Florence during Machiavelli's youth and who managed his fame so well that he is perhaps the one Italian ruler of Machiavelli's day whom many people know by name today—Lorenzo the Magnificent—though few could say why he was magnificent, or why he is still famous. For Lorenzo's wedding festivities in 1468, all sorts of spectacles were arranged—banquets, new dances, performances of ancient dramas, and more:

> Besides these things, in order to show further the greatness of the Medici house and of the state, there were two military spectacles. One, made up of men on horseback, represented a combat in the field; the other exhibited the storming of a town. These spectacles were carried on with the most extraordinary arrangement and *virtù* possible.

Later, under Lorenzo's rule, Machiavelli describes Florence as practiced in pageants, and he describes the city's young men as masters of fine appearance, whose "ambition was to appear magnificent in their clothing, and to use speech that was pithy and clever." When Machiavelli looks back at Lorenzo's life, he concludes that il Magnifico "kept his native city always celebrating festivities, in which jousts and representations of ancient deeds and triumphs were to be seen. His purpose was to keep the city rich, the people united, and the nobility honored."[19]

Yet, in these passages, there is more than a hint of criticism and satire, as in the comment on the dandified Florentine youths. The better the Medici rulers were at spectacles, the worse they seemed to be at the real events the spectacles mimicked. The shows put on by Piero to unite the people behind the government, despite their elaborateness, did not succeed: "After these shows had been presented, the citizens returned to their earlier thoughts, and each one followed his own opinion with more zeal than ever." The military spectacles at Lorenzo de' Medici's wedding festivities in 1468, "carried out with the most extraordinary arrangement and *virtù* possible," contrast with Florence's actual military ineptitude and lack of real *virtù* at this time. The two military spectacles—a combat in the field and the storming of a town—parallel two real Florentine adventures described by Machiavelli in the preceding pages: the ridiculous non-battle of Molinella in 1467, and the never-attained conquest of Lucca, the frustrated hope of Lorenzo's grandfather, Cosimo. In Machiavelli's narrative, real Florentine failures are depicted in Medici theater as images of triumph. The Florentine love of show and magnificence under Lorenzo, Machiavelli judges, were "customs contrary to all well-ordered commonwealths." They stemmed, he later makes plain, from the habits of Lorenzo himself: "he delighted in witty and keen men and in childish plays more than seemed fitting for so great a man."[20]

Machiavelli, it is well known, disdained the Medici yet felt the need to couch his disdain, for they dominated his political world (*The Prince* was dedicated first to Lorenzo's son and then his grandson, successive rulers of Florence). His comment in the *History of Florence* at the end of his encomium of Cosimo—"I have been obliged with an unusual method to praise him"—can be taken as a hint that he has shaped truth into a more pleasing fiction, rather than openly condemn the founder of the Medici regime.[21] Cosimo, so successful at quelling dissent in his own city, proved unable to achieve the vital Machiavellian political act, external conquest: it was an "affliction to the greatness of his spirit that he had not expanded Florentine territory with a conquest worthy of honor."[22] This lack of conquests, and more fundamentally the lack of real strength which would have made conquests possible, remained the fatal flaw of the Medici regime, as indeed for all the native actors in Machiavelli's Italy. The "battle" of Molinella staged so ludicrously during Piero de' Medici's rule by Florentine and Venetian mercenaries, and which Machiavelli alludes to ironically in his description of the mock battle at Lorenzo's wedding, is emblematic of the weakness of these Italian states. That Florence under the Medici was among the chief of these weak states serves more to condemn Medici rule than to praise it.

Piero's son Lorenzo, the last of the Medici princes whom Machiavelli treats in the *History of Florence*, was weak beneath an appearance of strength. Machiavelli had said that he won the tournament staged by his father not by favor but by his own worth, but Lorenzo admitted otherwise: "He himself confessed that he was not a hard hitter and won tournaments only because the judges wanted him to."[23] Machiavelli's own praise for Lorenzo carries an edge: when he concludes that Lorenzo's "wisdom and influence" made Italian arms "inactive," we should realize that rather than praising a peacemaker, he is condemning a foolish and harmful policy, especially in light of the chaos that came after Lorenzo. Lorenzo died in 1492, two years before the cataclysm of 1494, and the last sentence of the *History of Florence* links Lorenzo's end to the disaster's beginning: "No sooner was Lorenzo dead than Lodovico's ambition stimulated the growth of those evil seeds that not long after, since no living man could destroy them, devastated—and are still devastating—Italy."[24]

Machiavelli would seem to be praising Lorenzo by emphasizing the terrible consequences that followed his death, but one must read this seeming praise carefully. The true story is not the loss of Lorenzo's personal skill in balancing the states of Italy against each other but his failure to build up the strength of Florence and of Italy as a whole. As we have seen, Machiavelli says that this is the highest obligation of the ruler:

> It is not, then, the salvation of a republic or a kingdom to have a prince who will rule prudently while he lives, but to have one who will so organize it that even after he dies it can be maintained.[25]

Machiavelli, the most theatrical of political theorists, was well aware of the weakness and insufficiency of theater by itself. Or, as Machiavelli might observe, if you're going to spark an insurrection, you should go through with it.

(Though, in conditional rebuttal, if Donald Trump maintains his position as the leading Republican candidate for president in 2024 and manages to avoid a legal or political reckoning for the events of January 6, 2021, he may end up in position to teach even Machiavelli something about the unexpected possibilities of creative, must-watch political theater.)

Notes

1 From a commercial perspective, one might term such claims—a staple of Trump's oratory—"puffery," referring to advertising claims that are so lacking in factual foundation that a reasonable person should not them seriously. One article surveys a trio of jurisprudential definitions of puffery:

> The U.S. Court of Appeals for the Third Circuit . . . defines puffery as marketing "that is not deceptive, for no one would rely on its exaggerated claims."

> The Ninth Circuit describes puffery as "exaggerated advertising, blustering and boasting upon which no reasonable buyer would rely." Meanwhile, The Fifth Circuit defined puffery to be "a general claim of superiority over comparable products that is so vague that it can be understood as nothing more than a mere expression of opinion."

With "puffery," there is a sturdy legal tradition about marketing that claims of "greatest" and "biggest" and "best" are not meant to be taken as anything but expressions of opinion, and cannot be understood as lies in any meaningful sense.

2 *The Prince*, translated and edited by Harvey C. Mansfield, Jr. (Chicago: University of Chicago Press, 1985), ch. 18, p. 71.

3 Ibid., ch. 21, 88, 91; ch. 19, 78.

4 Ibid., ch. 18, 70.

5 Ibid., ch. 7, 29–30.

6 *History of Florence*, II.30, in Niccolò Machiavelli, *Machiavelli: The Chief Works and Others*, trans. and ed. Allan Gilbert, 3 vols. (Durham, N.C.: Duke University Press, 1965), p. 1115. (Subsequent citations from this edition of Machiavellli's works are denoted by 'G.')

7 Ibid., II.33, G 1122; II.34, G 1123.

8 Ibid., II.34, G 1123.

9 Ibid., II.35, G 1126.

10 Ibid., II.36, G 1127.

11 Ibid., II.36, G 1127–28.

12 Ibid., II.36, G 1129–30.

13 Ibid., II.37, G 1131.

14 Ibid., II.37, G 1133.

15 Ibid., III.16, G 1165.

16 Ibid., III.16–17, G 1166–68.

17 Ibid., III.7, G 1168.

18 Ibid., VII.12, G 1352.

19 Ibid., VII.21, G 1364–65 (Gilbert translates *virtù* as "excellence" here); VII.28, G 1372; VIII.36, G 1433 (Gilbert translates *rappresentazioni* as "presentations").

20 Ibid., VII.12, G 1352; VII.28, G 1372; VII.36, G 1434.

21 Ibid., VII.6, G 1346. Machiavelli rewrote passages in the *History of Florence* to make them less critical of Cosimo: see Gilbert's introduction, G 1027–28. The fictive quality of the genre of the "mirror of princes," which Machiavelli says he has followed in praising Cosimo, is well known. It is one of the reasons Xenophon's *Cyropaedia* has often been dismissed as a romance and its political aspect disregarded (and one of the reasons Sir Philip Sidney saw it as the classic instance of the poet's "feigning," and made it the centerpiece of his *Defence of Poesy*).

22 *History of Florence*, VII.6, G 1345.

23 Anthony Grafton, "Humanism and Political Theory," in J. H. Burns (ed.), *The Cambridge History of Political Thought 1450–1700* (Cambridge: Cambridge University Press, 1991), 28.

24 *History of Florence*, VIII.36, G 1432–34. Lodovico was the Duke of Milan, whose machinations after Lorenzo's death encouraged the entry of the French king into Italy.

25 *The Discourses*, I.11, G 226.

6

POPULISM FROM ABOVE

Donald Trump, Andrew Jackson, and the Politics of White Vengeance

J.M. Opal

On March 15, 2017, President Donald J. Trump did something out of character: He praised someone other than himself as a great leader. While visiting the Hermitage, the former home of Andrew Jackson near Nashville, Tennessee, Mr. Trump called Jackson "the people's president," the champion of ordinary citizens versus corrupt elites. Jackson had protected workers with tariffs and stood up for everyday people, Trump declared. Addressing Old Hickory's spirit via Twitter, Trump continued: "We thank you for your service. We honor your memory. We build on your legacy and we thank God for the USA!" In a subsequent interview, the new President praised Jackson as a "swashbuckler," who might have prevented the Civil War.[1]

Historians quickly fact-checked these statements, noting that the opposition Whigs, not Jackson's Democrats, had fought for protective tariffs during the 1830s and also that Jackson had died in 1845, sixteen years before the start of the Civil War. They scoffed at Trump's swaggering ignorance. But, as usual, the self-promoting billionaire and reality TV star had made his point loudly and quickly, defining the terms in which he would be discussed. Donald Trump, the 45th President, wanted people to liken him to Andrew Jackson, the 7th President. So, he made clear that he saw himself as Jackson reborn. Sure enough, the dominant media narrative during the summer of 2017 named both Trump and Jackson as two-of-a-kind "populists." This in turn led to much confusion about populism itself.[2]

This confusion was inevitable, because while all populists reject "elites," they identify those elites in contradictory ways. Right-leaning populists name government officials and career politicians as the enemy elites. To this way of thinking, elites are *only* found in government, within a political class who stand apart from "the people." This enables right-wing populists, most of whom are

DOI: 10.4324/9781003110361-6

wealthy businessmen, to make common cause with certain segments of the middle and working classes. By contrast, left-leaning populists see elites more in private enterprise than in public service. They trace the people's ills more to capitalism than to democracy. One kind of populist tends to think that society has become too permissive and forgiving, whereas the other sees society itself as cruel and unjust. One yearns for a golden past where people like them were in charge, whereas the other imagines a more decent future where everyone gets his due.

By the end of 2017, as the Jackson comparisons began to die down, Trump had shown which kind of populist he was. Yet having drawn the parallel with Jackson, Trump continued to benefit from it. With Jackson's portrait looking on from the Oval Office, Americans kept puzzling over what the business tycoon in the White House *really* wanted, as if they were afraid of questioning Jackson's sincerity along with Trump's. Did the new President secretly identify with blue-collar workers in the Rust Belt, even though he was frantically appointing right-wing federal judges who despised unions? Did he genuinely seek to turn the Republicans into the "party of the American worker," even after signing a massive tax cut for the wealthy? When the populist label failed to show how Trump might be like Jackson, many wondered about a more personal link between the two men. Did Trump and Jackson have similar instincts? Did they share a leadership style? Or did the connection run deeper still, into their fundamental beliefs about America and its enemies?

As of this writing, Trump is fading somewhat from the national spotlight, enabling greater perspective on his comparison with Jackson. In many respects, that comparison now looks absurd. Andrew Jackson came from a humble but respectable background and then followed a career path similar to other ambitious young men in post-Revolutionary America. He made his name as a lawyer, judge, and federal official in the Southwest Territory (present-day Tennessee) during the 1780s and 1790s. He strongly opposed popular demands for debt relief and showed limited interest in democratic reform. By the time he ran for President in the mid-1820s, Jackson had helped to write a state constitution, served twice in the US Congress, and led US military operations from New Orleans to Pensacola. He even chaired the Committee on Military Affairs during his brief Senate term from 1822 to 1824. In all these ways, Andrew Jackson was ready to become President in 1829 and resembled future general-statesmen such as William Henry Harrison, Ulysses S. Grant, and even Dwight D. Eisenhower.[3]

Donald Trump had no military background and no experience in public office when he began his run at the White House in 2015. He was radically unprepared for the office he won the following year. The differences with Jackson were just as profound in terms of personality and character. Jackson was intensely moralistic and self-denying. Both he and his wife Rachel prayed to an unforgiving Presbyterian God who cast sinful people and nations into hellfire. They sought guidance in the historic books of the Old Testament and the Book of Revelations, which concludes with apocalyptic warfare between the Godly and satanic. For his part, Trump was cartoonish in his lechery and barely able to name any part of the Bible. Jackson was extremely private, whereas Trump's seedy antics filled the tabloids. Jackson was recklessly brave, risking his body with almost suicidal abandon. Trump let others fight his battles, right up to the moment on January 6, 2021, when he slunk back to the White House to watch his angry mob sack the Capitol.[4]

In one crucial respect, however, these two men saw eye to eye. "Get even with people," Trump told an audience in 2011. "If they screw you, screw them back 10 times as hard. I really believe it." He never forgot an insult, and he nursed grudges even against the dead. So did Jackson. "An Eye for an Eye, Toothe for Toothe, and Scalp for Scalp," he warned a Spanish official in Florida during the War of 1812. "*You know me*," he later told a friend. "I will curb my feelings until it becomes proper to act," whereupon he would take "retributive *Justice*." This shared desire for vengeance came out of a worldview in which only the strong survived, a grim and even paranoid *mentalité* in which weakness of any kind invited mistreatment and disgrace. As they rose to power during two very different periods, Jackson and Trump mingled their deep belief in retribution with an equally vivid sense that "the people," by which they meant white Americans, had suffered too long. This gave them an electric hold over their followers but quite different legacies in American political history.[5]

Men on the Make

Legend has it that Jackson was born in a frontier cabin, poor and proud. This is roughly true but also misleading. His parents emigrated from northern Ireland to South Carolina in 1765, then bought a plot of land near his maternal uncles in a settlement known as the Waxhaws, which spread over the ill-defined boundary with North Carolina. His father died while his mother Betty was pregnant with him, her third son. This family grew up far from the urban center of Charleston, to say nothing of the imperial center of London. But the Waxhaws were prosperous, and Betty had five sisters in the settlement, two of whom were married to prominent men. One of Andrew's uncles owned lands and slaves in North Carolina while also holding a militia title in South Carolina. Such men had no quarrel with the ruling elites of Charleston, except insofar as Westerners had to travel to the seaport to pursue criminals or debtors. Indeed, a vigilante movement known as the South Carolina Regulation broke out just after Jackson's birth in 1767. For several years, propertied men in the region took violent action against the "shocking Outrages" of mixed-race criminals and alleged prostitutes.[6]

Andrew was a quick study, and his pious mother wanted to make a Presbyterian minister of him. According to the religious traditions she passed on, the virtuous settlers of northern Ireland had relived the trials of the ancient Israelites by bringing light to dark places through toil and bloodshed. Just a few years after he began to prepare for this calling, however, Andrew's world darkened as the King's armies approached. In late 1780 and early 1781, Jackson watched his boyhood church go up in flames and suffered a blow to the head from the Loyalist or British officer who took him and his one surviving brother as prisoners. Soon after, this brother died of smallpox, while his mother never returned from a trip to Charleston. She was as brave as a lion, he liked to say. He often narrated his life as a series of devotions to the faith she had placed in him.[7]

Orphaned by the war and impatient of authority, the young Jackson realized that the way to wealth and prominence—"honor," as he preferred—was the law, not the ministry. He tried his first case in 1788 in western North Carolina, challenging his more experienced opponent to a duel after the older lawyer disdained him. "[You] have insulted me in the presence of a court and a large audienc[e]," Jackson seethed. He then moved two hundred miles west to a new settlement around Nashville, bringing with him an enslaved woman named Nancy as well as news of the ratification of the US Constitution. He served as Attorney General in the Southwest Territory as well as a private attorney for the region's creditors. He allied himself with the territory's Governor, William Blount, who was one of the most well-connected men in all of North Carolina and Tennessee.[8]

In these ways, Jackson was a southern and western version of Alexander Hamilton, a talented and hyper-ambitious young man who rose by embracing the new institutions of federal law and modern commerce. He was driven but dutiful, headstrong but ultimately respectful of those in power. And he was scrupulous, if not always successful in private dealings. When his import–export business sputtered in 1804, a victim of fickle prices for the great new staple of cotton, Jackson swore that he would pay his debts even if it involved him "in all the calamity of poverty." That year he sold his first plantation to satisfy "the principles of Justice to [his] creditors" and moved his wife into a smaller home called Rural Retreat, later renamed the Hermitage.[9]

It is hard to imagine a greater contrast with Donald Trump. Born into a millionaire's family in Queens in 1946, at the start of the Baby Boom, Trump looked up to his bullying father but otherwise had little need of family duties. In fact, he showed no interest in duties of any kind, avoiding military service in Vietnam with a fictional foot injury. Leveraging his birthright, he became President of the Trump Management Company in 1974 and hit his stride as a brash Manhattan entrepreneur during the greed-is-good era of Ronald Reagan. He bought casinos in Atlantic City, a palatial hotel in New York, and even a short-lived airline—all of them splattered with his ideophonic last name.[10]

Beyond the properties he marketed, Trump sold a fantasy: That anyone who stepped into his casinos could be as rich and famous as he was, if only while they kept their wallets open. In fact, Trump lived inside the mirage he trafficked. His core businesses hemorrhaged money even in the booming 1980s, and when the real estate markets dove in 1990, he narrowly avoided personal bankruptcy. By 1991, his two-year losses totaled $517.5 million. For most of the next twenty years, he cashed in on his gilded name, promising everyone from readers of his book, *The Art of the Deal* (1987) to students at the so-called Trump University (2005–2010) that he knew the secrets of success.[11]

By his own admission, Trump used corporate bankruptcy laws to maximum advantage, leaving his creditors with as few crumbs as possible. Court records also indicate that his businesses routinely stiffed vendors and small contractors. In the long American tradition of carnival barkers and traveling showmen, Donald Trump kept just ahead of the angry locals to whom he had sold a bill of goods. His personal life followed a similar path. He divorced his first wife, the model Ivana Marie Zelǹicková, in 1991, after months of headlines about his affair with another model, Marla Maples. Trump and Maples were married for four years, after which he met a third model, Melania Knauss. Trump and Knauss wed in 2005, the same year he told an *Access Hollywood* reporter about his romantic strategy ("Grab them by the pussy") and one year before an alleged tryst with adult film star Stormy Daniels.[12]

Nationalists

If Andrew Jackson's constitutional and economic values aligned with the right-thinking Federalists who remade the United States with the Constitution of 1787, one episode from the Tennessee frontiers alienated him from those founders. Beginning in September 1792, war parties of militant young Chickamauga and Creek men struck the thin line of white settlements around Nashville and Knoxville. They targeted both forts and homesteads. About 30% of the victims were women and children, and the region's only newspaper, the *Knoxville Gazette*, printed graphic details of the mangled bodies of defenseless and often pregnant white women. "[She was found] in a most indecent posture—thus insulting the sex, insulting human nature," the paper reported of one victim. "The stain made by the blood of [her unborn baby] . . . cannot be washed out, but by the blood of the whole Cherokee nation."[13]

As a territorial official, Andrew Jackson was often far from Nashville during this long nightmare. He left Rachel at home with their three slaves. On August 29, 1793, for example, he narrowly escaped an ambush at a fort south of Knoxville, some 180 miles from his home. Jackson himself managed to escape and alert "the whole frontier," the *Gazette* reported, only to find that the Washington administration prevented white riders from pursuing Indian attackers south of the Tennessee River. The following May, Jackson despaired that the Nashville settlement might not survive the summer. That September, he almost certainly took part in an expedition to two Chickamauga towns, Running Water and Nickajack. The white attackers burned these villages and killed all who fled, forcing the Chickamaugans to terms.[14]

After sitting in Tennessee's constitutional convention in 1796, Jackson briefly served in the US Congress, refusing a vote of thanks to George Washington. His political fortunes then waned along with his business ventures until war broke out again in 1812. After a group of Creek radicals known as Redsticks kidnapped a midwife along a river south of Nashville, Jackson called for collective retribution on guilty blood. "This cruel outrage must not go unrevenged," he told the governor. To muster volunteers, he invoked "the celebrated expedition against Nick-a-Jack," and in early 1814, his mixed force of Tennessee militiamen and US soldiers wiped out a Redstick stronghold in northern Alabama. "We have seen the ravens and vultures preying upon the carcasses of the unburied slain," he told his troops. This made Jackson famous in the western and southern states where native attack and slave insurrection were constant fears. "The BLOOD of our citizens cry loud for VENGEANCE," a St. Louis newspaper declared in May 1814 after a body washed up along the Missouri River. "The general cry is let the north as well as the south be JACKSONISED!!!" Early the next year, Jackson stopped a British invasion force bound for New Orleans, becoming the most beloved American general since Washington.[15]

Even as the United States and Great Britain made peace, Jackson panted for vengeance against the native and Black fighters who had fled to Spanish Florida. Acting without clear authorization, Jackson invaded Florida in early 1818 with another mixed force of militia and US regulars, destroying all the Seminole and Black settlements in his path. To his pious wife back in Tennessee, Jackson reported that he had taken the "Just Vengeance of heaven" on dark, guilty places and dark, sinful nations. In early 1819, Congress investigated his actions in Florida, and while a minority denounced him for ignoring constitutional and international law, most praised him as the "great avenger" of a nation long victimized by semi-demonic foes. One Congressman even took on the voice of a murdered Georgia woman, who looked down to warn the fallen world "that there is avenging God."[16]

To some extent, Donald Trump's fame followed a similar trajectory: A dramatic rise around 1980, much like Jackson's ascent around 1790, followed by a long period of relative decline. And while Jackson turned things around with his military victories, Donald Trump entered politics with war-like rhetoric. In 1989, he took out a full-page advertisement in several New York papers after unknown attackers beat and raped a white woman jogging in Central Park. "Bring Back the Death Penalty. Bring Back Our Police!" the headline screamed. Trump declared that the five young suspects (four Blacks and one Latino) should be "forced to suffer." In later TV interviews on the subject, he said that these and other criminals enjoyed "unbelievable rights," while victims had none. The people were "tired, sick and tired" of milquetoast politicians and liberal apologists. He never apologized for these comments after DNA evidence exonerated the "Central Park Five."[17]

Trump half-heartedly ran for President on the "reform" ticket in 2000, claiming that the world was kicking America around. He played a business tycoon on *The Apprentice* and talked about his strategies for "surviving at the top." Then, in 2008, Barack Obama was elected president amidst a global economic crisis and a disastrous war in Iraq. Within months, a far-right movement called the Tea Party claimed that Obama had raised their taxes to bail out undeserving homeowners. Overwhelmingly white and middle-class, Tea Party members spread wild theories about Obama as an anti-colonial African, a stealth Bolshevik, and a closet Muslim. Aided by new forms of conservative media, the Tea Party took over much of the Republican Party after powering big GOP gains in the 2010 midterm elections.[18]

Trump saw his opening. By early 2011, he was one of the loudest voices in the so-called Birther movement, which posited that Obama had been born in Kenya and was thus ineligible to serve as president. This charge resonated with those who could not bear the sight of a Black family in the White House. "He doesn't have a birth certificate, or if he does, there's something on that certificate that is very bad for him," he told *Fox News* in March. Trump suggested that "something" was evidence of Muslim birth. Such statements made Trump extremely popular not only with the Tea Party but also with fringe elements of the far right, including neo-fascist groups like the Three Percenters and former KKK leader David Duke.[19]

The Faithful

Even Jackson's critics during the 1819 debate over the Florida invasion praised his service to the nation. Unmoved, Jackson cursed these congressmen as corrupt ingrates and moved back to friendlier ground in Tennessee, only to find a new democratic movement taking form in the midst of economic crisis. This "Relief" movement called for debt relief and public banks—anathema to Jackson's archconservative economic and legal principles. Even when the more radical voices of this movement died down, a new popular party led by one of Jackson's former lieutenants took over the state government in early 1821. Jackson saw this man, too, as an ungrateful "monster" and a threat to the "respectability" of Tennessee. Within months, Jackson and his circle of elite planters and lawyers in Nashville were planning his presidential campaign.[20]

As a step to the White House, Jackson served in the US Senate from 1822 to 1824. There he carved out a moderate ground except on matters of national vengeance: He was one of only six Senators to vote for military action against the Blackfeet and Arikara nations on the northwestern frontier as well as against

South American pirates on Caribbean islands. "You must cause vengeance to reach them," one Jacksonian Senator said of Caribbean pirates. Collective retribution on pirate strongholds like Cuba was the only way to avenge "the blood of our people." In the 1824 presidential race, Jackson fell short after a disputed election in which the winner, John Quincy Adams, allegedly made a "Corrupt Bargain" with the most powerful man in Congress, Henry Clay. This reinforced the Jacksonian message that the people—and their champion—had been patient and forbearing for too long and so deserved revenge.[21]

As the election of 1828 neared, Jackson could count on southern support. His actions from his time in Tennessee during the 1790s to his attack on Florida in 1818 revealed his single-minded pursuit of more lands ruled by white cotton planters and "unmixed by Indians." His extreme hostility to indigenous nations and rebellious slaves made him a hero to the great majority of white southerners. North of slavery, however, Jackson's economic vision was not so obvious, his national priorities not so clear. Did he support Henry Clay's new proposals for an "American System" of high tariffs and internal improvements? Or was he a southerner in his economic and foreign policy as well, a proponent of "free trade" in slave-grown cotton and of mass exports to Europe?[22]

Jackson's handlers focused on Pennsylvania, then as now a battleground state. Most of the Pennsylvanians wanted to develop their country through better infrastructures and protective tariffs. Jackson had other priorities, so his campaign changed the subject. The leading pro-Jackson pamphlet in the state was *The Letters of Wyoming*, a reference to the Wyoming Valley of central Pennsylvania, where in 1778 Loyalist and Indian marauders had slaughtered white settlers. Voting for Jackson, "the old Hero," was a way to redeem the blood and memory of those lost to the nation's savage and demonic foes. Carried by "Hickory Clubs" who rallied voters across the state, this message gave Jackson 67% of the vote in the Keystone State. With this foothold in the North and his overwhelming popularity in the slave states, Jackson cruised to electoral victory.[23]

Almost two centuries later, Donald Trump also counted on the southern vote while courting Pennsylvania and the Rust Belt. Breaking with other GOP leaders, he denounced free trade deals that enabled US companies to shift operations to cheap-labor countries like Mexico. He promised to bring back factory and mining jobs, and he signaled that he would not touch Social Security and Medicare, which the more fanatical right-wingers in the GOP sought to privatize. Yet too much can be made of Trump's deviations from conservative economic ideas. In his stated hostility to taxes, regulations, and unions, not to mention "socialism" and "big government," Trump was a regular Republican. What set him apart, in Pennsylvania and elsewhere, was his willingness to speak directly to white racial resentments—to call, in effect, for white vengeance against a range of threats from non-white people at home and abroad.[24]

In his first speech as a presidential contender, Trump denounced immigrants from Mexico for "bringing their problems" to the United States. "They're bringing crime, they're bringing drugs, they're rapists." He also called for the construction of a "great, great wall" along the southern border. Thereafter, Trump rallies routinely erupted in chants of "Build the Wall!" Following a mass shooting by ISIS sympathizers in San Bernardino, California in December 2015, Trump called for a "total and complete shutdown" on Muslims entering the United States. (This proposal might not be politically correct, he told a rapturous crowd in South Carolina, but "I don't care.") The implication here was that the white American majority was in *actual* danger, not just of political decline but also of physical harm from Mexicans and Muslims.[25]

Trump doubled down on these themes after he bested the other GOP candidates and accepted the party's nomination in July 2016. He weaved in attacks on free trade deals but framed his message around violence and retribution. "The attacks on our police, and the terrorism in our cities, threaten our way life." Citing recent shootings of police officers in Texas and Louisiana, he devised a figure of 180,000 illegal aliens with criminal records, "roaming free to threaten peaceful citizens." After his stunning victory over Hillary Clinton that November, he gave one of the darkest Inauguration speeches in American history. "The American carnage stops right here, right now." Even in his half-hearted gesture to racial harmony, Trump struck a graphic note: "We all bleed the same red blood of patriotism."[26]

Promises Kept

Once in office, Andrew Jackson used every means at his disposal to deport roughly 50,000 Creeks, Cherokees, Choctaws, and Chickasaws from the Deep South. To do so, he defied native resistance, a massive anti-Removal campaign in northern states, and a Supreme Court decision. Mostly he enabled state authorities and private militias to do the dirty work, although his Secretary of War quickly dispatched troops when some Creeks rebelled in 1835, and his handpicked successor as President, Martin Van Buren, oversaw a full-scale war to remove the Seminole from northern Florida. Cotton production surged as white settlers and speculators poured into the stolen ground, and slaveholders from the old tobacco lands of Virginia and Maryland now grew rich by selling people "down the river" to Mississippi and Louisiana.[27]

As for Trump, he immediately signed an Executive Order banning travel from seven majority-Muslim countries into the United States. At the end of his first year in office, he delivered a massive tax cut. In return for weaker public services from cash-strapped governments, middle-class households thus received a brief and modest reduction in taxes, whereas the most affluent Americans took in huge and growing windfalls, most notably through the near elimination of the estate tax. His administration shredded labor and environmental regulations and appointed anti-labor, far-right federal judges at frantic speed. He only managed to build 15 miles of new border wall along the 2,000-mile United

States–Mexico line, but he curtailed border crossing with draconian policies such as the forced separation of migrant children from their parents.[28]

When Trump declared himself to be Jackson reincarnated, then, he pointed to an authentic commonality between himself and Old Hickory. Both led political movements animated, in large part, by a specific narrative of white grievance and a particular demand for white vengeance. In Jackson's time, this politics came out of decades of harrowing struggle against native peoples, Black slaves, and their occasional allies in the British Empire. In the era of Trump, this politics reflected the rise of a more multi-racial culture, which began with the Civil Rights movements and liberal immigration laws of the 1960s and culminated in the election of Barack Obama in 2008. Both Jackson and Trump had passionate followers, who correctly saw these men as true believers who would deliver what they promised: A kind of populism from above, in which white men like them could more fully dominate America.

Just as these two men came out of very different backgrounds, however, they also came to power in very different contexts. In the early 1800s, the political power of ordinary white men was growing alongside the national sense of victimization. Colonial and revolutionary-era restrictions on the right to vote fell apart, so that by the time Jackson took office in 1829, only a handful of the 24 states retained property qualifications. Everywhere else, the so-called Age of the Common Man had already begun. Despite his conservative legal and economic beliefs, Jackson did not fight these political trends. To the contrary, he took them on as his own, as when calling for the abolition of the Electoral College after his 1824 defeat. During his second term, he confronted the Second Bank of the United States, arguing that it benefited wealthy foreigners, and in his retirement, he praised an effort to abolish voting restrictions in Rhode Island. Jackson had nothing to fear from majorities, and so he embraced them.[29]

Whereas Jackson's brand of right-wing populism acquired something of the burgeoning democracy of the age, Trump's call to Make America Great Again resonated with white voters whose demographic and cultural weight was in decline. When Donald Trump first considered running for President in 2000, non-Hispanic whites made up 76% of the nation's electorate. By 2018, two years after Trump first lost the popular vote, that figure had fallen to 68%, with declines in all 50 states and double-digit drops in ten of them. By the time Trump lost the popular vote for the second time in November 2020, this time by over seven million votes, white voters made up only 65% of the electorate. They voted strongly for Trump, just as they had in 2016, but they could no longer overcome the even stronger opposition of every other group.[30]

At no time during his four years in office did Trump's approval rating break 45%, and when he left Washington on January 21, 2021, two weeks after several hundred of his most violent supporters invaded the US Capitol, just 38% approved of his tenure. (A startling number of the Capitol rioters came from regions where the white population was in fast decline.) Almost half of

Americans felt that Trump would be remembered as one of the worst presidents in history. Here, then, is the ultimate reason that Donald Trump compared himself to Andrew Jackson: Old Hickory was far more popular than The Donald ever was. And while the slaveholding soldier from the Carolina borderlands could accept democracy and even advance a violent and racist form of it, the dodgy tycoon from Queens can only hope that his endless lies about the 2020 election will yet break America's flawed but deep democratic traditions.[31]

Notes

1 Holly Meyer and Joel Ebert, "Trump Tours the Hermitage, Lays Wreath on Andrew Jackson's Tomb," *The Tennessean*, March 15, 2017; Zach Schonfeld, "Understanding Trump's Weird Obsession with Andrew Jackson," *Newsweek*, May 1, 2017.

2 Jonathan Capeheart, "Donald Trump's Woeful Ignorance about the Civil War and Andrew Jackson," *The Chicago Tribune*, May 1, 2017; DeNeen L. Brown, "Trump Called Andrew Jackson a 'Swashbuckler.' The Cherokees Called Him, 'Indian Killer'," *The Washington Post*, May 3, 2017; J. M. Opal, "Why the Donald Trump-Andrew Jackson Bromance is Bad for America," *New York Daily News*, May 1, 2017.

3 Hendrik Booream, *Young Hickory: The Making of Andrew Jackson* (Dallas: Taylor Trade, 2001); Andrew Burstein, *The Passions of Andrew Jackson* (New York: Alfred A. Knopf, 2003); Mark R. Cheathem, *Andrew Jackson, Southerner* (Baton Rouge: Louisiana State University Press, 2013); J. M. Opal, *Avenging the People: Andrew Jackson, the Rule of Law, and the American Nation* (New York: Oxford University Press, 2017).

4 Jessica Taylor, "Citing 'Two Corinthians,' Trump Struggles to Make the Sale to Evangelicals," *National Public Radio: Vermont Public Radio*, January 18, 2016, www.npr.org/2016/01/18/463528847/citing-two-corinthians-trump-struggles-to-make-the-sale-to-evangelicals.

5 David Corn, "Donald Trump is Completely Obsessed with Revenge," *Mother Jones*, October 19, 2016; Andrew Jackson to Mateo Gonzáles Manrique, 24 August 1814, in *Papers of Andrew Jackson*, ed. Daniel Feller et al. (Knoxville: University of Tennessee, 1988–), 3: 121, hereafter *PAJ*; AJ to Samuel Houston, 15 December 1826, in *PAJ* 6: 243.

6 Charles Woodmason, "Copy of a Presented to the Commons House of Assembly of South Carolina," [November 1767], in *The Carolina Backcountry on the Eve of the Revolution: The Journal and Other Writings of Charles Woodmason, Anglican Itinerant*, ed. Richard Hooker (Chapel Hill: University of North Carolina Press, 1953), 214.

7 T.C. Barnard, "The Uses of 23 October 1641 and Irish Protestant Celebrations," *English Historical Review*, vol. 106 (October 1991), 889–920; "Jackson's Description of His Experiences During and Immediately Following the Revolutionary War," *PAJ*, 1:5.

8 AJ to Waightstill Avery, 12 August 1788, in *PAJ* 1:12. William Blount's commercial and political empire is revealed in *The John Gray Blount Papers*, ed. Alice Barnwell Keith and William H. Masterson (3 vols., Raleigh: Division of Archives and History, Department of Cultural Resources, 1952–65).

9 AJ to Rachel Jackson, 6 April 1804, in *PAJ* 2:13 and AJ to Thomas and John Clifford, 24 July 1804, in *PAJ* 2:28.

10 George Beahm, *Trump Talk: Donald Trump in His Own Words* (New York: Mendel Media Group LLC, 2016); David Patterson, *Grand Expectations: The United States, 1945–1974* (New York: Oxford University Press, 1996), 77–81.

11 John Cassidy, "Donald Trump's Business Failures Were Very Real," *The New Yorker*, May 10, 2019; "Trump University: Court Upholds $25m Settlement to Give Students' Money Back," *The Guardian*, February 6, 2018; Chris Hedges, "Trump, the Quintessential American," *Truthdig*, December 17, 2018.
12 Clare O'Conner, "Fourth Time's a Charm: How Donald Trump Made Bankruptcy Work For Him," *Forbes*, April 29, 2011; Alexandra Berzon, "Donald Trump's Business Plan Left a Trail of Unpaid Bills," *Wall Street Journal*, June 9, 2016; Kate Taylor, "Stormy Daniels is Taking a Victory Lap after Michael Cohen's Guilty Plea," *Business Insider*, August 25, 2018.
13 "[To] Mr. Roulston," *Knoxville Gazette*, 13 August 1793; "A List of the Names of Persons Killed, Murdered, and Captured Since the 26th of February 1794," *Knoxville Gazette*, 11 October 1794; Carroll Smith-Rosenberg, *This Violent Empire: The Birth of an American National Identity* (Chapel Hill: The University of North Carolina Press, 2010); Peter Silver, *Our Savage Neighbors: How Indian War Transformed Early America* (New York: W.W. Norton and Company, 2008).
14 "Knoxville," *Knoxville Gazette*, 14 September 1793; AJ to John McKee, 16 May 1794, PAJ 1:49; Opal, *Avenging the People*, 76–104.
15 AJ to Willie Blount, 5 June 1812, in *PAJ* 2: 301; [AJ], "The Massacre at the Mouth of the Duck River," *Democratic Clarion*, 7 July 1812, in *PAJ* 2: 311, 310; "St. Louis," *Missouri Gazette and Illinois Advertiser*, 28 May 1814; Tom Kanon, *Tennesseans at War, 1812–1815: Andrew Jackson, The Creek War, and the Battle of New Orleans* (Tuscaloosa: University of Alabama Press, 2014); David S. Heidler and Jeanne T. Heidler, *Old Hickory's War: Andrew Jackson and the Quest for Empire* (Baton Rouge: The Louisiana State University Press, 2003).
16 AJ letter to Rachel Jackson quoted in Burstein, *Passions of Andrew Jackson*, 218–19; Opal, *Avenging the People*, 170 ("great avenger"), 169 ("avenging God), and 164–71; Deborah A. Rosen, *Border Law: The First Seminole War and American Nationhood* (Cambridge, MA: Harvard University Press, 2015).
17 Oliver Laughland, "Donald Trump and the Central Park Five: The Racially Charged Rise of a Demagogue," *The Guardian*, 17 February 2016; J.M. Opal, "The Historical Roots of Trump's Anger with Canada," *The Walrus*, 25 June 2018.
18 Christopher S. Parker and Matt A. Barreto, *Change They Can't Believe In: The Tea Party and Reactionary Politics in America* (Princeton: Princeton University Press, 2013), 191–217; Anthony DiMaggio, *The Rise of the Tea Party: Political Discontent and Corporate Media in the Age of Obama* (New York: Monthly Review Press, 2011).
19 Gregory Krieg, "14 of Trump's Most Outrageous 'Birther' Claims—Half from After 2011," *CNN*, 16 September 2016; Ta-Nehisi Coates, "The First White President," *The Atlantic*, October 2017.
20 AJ to John Coffee, 2 February 1816, in *PAJ* 4:7 (describing William Carroll, the future Governor, and his friends as "monsters"); AJ to John Coffee, 26 July 1821, in *PAJ* 5:83; David S. Heidler and Jeanne T. Heidler, *The Rise of Andrew Jackson: Myth, Manipulation, and the Making of Modern Politics* (New York: Basic Books, 2018).
21 Jackson ally Philip Barbour quoted in Opal, *Avenging the People*, 196; Donald B. Cole, *Vindicating Andrew Jackson: The 1828 Election and the Rise of the Two Party System* (Lawrence: University of Kansas Press, 2009); Lynn Hudson Parsons, *The Birth of Modern Politics: Andrew Jackson, John Quincy Adams, and the Election of 1828* (New York: Oxford University Press, 2009).
22 AJ to John Williams, 18 May 1814, in *PAJ* 3:75; Daniel Peart, "Looking Beyond Parties and Elections: The Making of United States Tariff Policy during the Early 1820s," *Journal of the Early Republic*, vol. 33 (Spring 2013), 87–108; James L. Huston,

"Virtue Besieged: Virtue, Equality, and the General Welfare in the Tariff Debates of the 1820s," *Journal of the Early Republic*, vol. 14 (Winter 1994), 523–547.

23 Robert P. Hay, "The Case for Andrew Jackson in 1824: Eaton's *Wyoming Letters*," *Tennessee Historical Quarterly*, vol. 29 (Summer 1970), 139–151; Michael J. Dubin, *United States Presidential Elections, 1788–1860: The Official Results by County and State* (Jefferson, NC: McFarland and Company, 2002), 48.

24 Mugambi Jouet, *Exceptional America: What Divides Americans from the World and from Each Other* (Oakland: University of California Press, 2017), 168–93.

25 Jeremy Diamond, "Donald Trump: Ban All Muslim Travel to U.S.," *CNN.com*, 8 December 2015; Diamond, "Trump Supporters Embrace Muslim Travel Ban Plan," *CNN.com*, 7 December 2015.

26 "Full Text: Donald Trump 2016 RNC Draft Speech Transcript," *Politico*, 21 July 2016; "Inaugural Address: Trump's Full Speech," *CNN.com*, 21 January 2017; Glenn Kessler and Michelle Ye Hee Lee, "Fact-checking Donald Trump's Acceptance Speech at the 2016 RNC," *Washington Post*, 21 July 2016.

27 Ethan Davis, "An Administrative Trail of Tears: Indian Removal," *American Journal of Legal History*, vol. 50 (January 2008–2010), 49–100; Seth Rockman, "Jacksonian America," in *American History Now*, ed. Eric Foner and Lisa McGirr (Philadelphia: Temple University Press, 2011), 52–74; Daniel Feller, *The Public Lands in Jacksonian Politics, 1815–1840* (Madison: University of Wisconsin Press, 1984); Walter Johnson, *River of Dark Dreams: Slavery and Empire in the Cotton Kingdom* (Cambridge, MA: Harvard University Press, 2013).

28 Abed Ayoub and Khaled Beydoun, "Executive Disorder: The Muslim Ban, Emergency Advocacy, and the Fires Next Time," *Michigan Journal of Race and Law*, vol. 22 (2017), 215–41; Ben Steverman, Dave Merrill, and Jeremy C.F. Lin, "A Year After the Middle Class Tax Cut, the Rich are Winning," *Bloomberg*, 18 December 2018; Ian Millhiser, "What Trump Has Done to the Courts, Explained," *Vox*, 29 September 2020; Lucy Rodgers and Dominic Bailey, "Trump Wall: How Much Has He Actually Built?" *BBC News*, 31 October 2020; Franco Ordoñez, "Task Force Investigates Whether Trump Separated Families Earlier than Known," *National Public Radio*, 7 April 2021.

29 Sean Wilentz, *The Rise of American Democracy: Jefferson to Lincoln* (New York: W.W. Norton and Company, 2005).

30 Ruth Igielnik and Abby Budiman, "The Changing Racial and Ethnic Composition of the U.S. Electorate," *Pew Research Center*, 23 September 2020; Fabiola Cineas and Anna North, "We Need to Talk about the White People Who Voted for Donald Trump," *Vox*, 7 November 2020; Dante Chinni, "Did Biden Win by a Little or a Lot? The Answer is . . . Yes," *NBCNews.com*, 20 December 2020.

31 Laura Santhanam, "Trump Will Be Remembered as One of the Worst U.S. Presidents, Nearly Half of Americans Say," *PBSNewsHour, pbs.org*, 19 January 2021; "How Unpopular is Donald Trump?" *FiveThirtyEight*, 21 January 2021; Robert A. Pape, "What an Analysis of 377 Americans Arrested or Charged in the Capitol Insurrection Tells Us," *The Washington Post*, 6 April 2021.

7

IDOLS OF CONSUMPTION

From Mussolini to Trump

Simonetta Falasca-Zamponi

In a chapter, first published in 1944 and later reprinted with the evocative title "The Triumph of Mass Idols," renowned Frankfurt scholar Leo Löwenthal discussed the astounding changes that had transformed the genre of biography since the turn of the century.[1] A new phenomenon in its own right, especially in the years following World War I, biographies had become a staple feature of popular magazines and a booming sensation on the book market. Coveted profiles of Bismarck, Goethe, and Napoleon by the likes of the German-Swiss author Emil Ludwig sold millions of copies and were translated in multiple languages. The sign of a rising public interest in individuals' private lives, the success of biographies during the first part of the 1900s rebounded in the American popular press, with sections of periodicals regularly dedicated to the portrayal of singular characters' stories. Considering the magnitude of the phenomenon and with the aim of addressing its effects, Löwenthal engaged in a content analysis study that looked at biographies printed from March 1941 to April 1942 in two popular magazines: *The Saturday Evening Post* and *Collier's*. Incidentally, a preliminary historical survey of the two weeklies from the beginning of the century provided him with the most invaluable finding and an initial clue to his intellectual conundrum: biographers' preferred subjects had shifted over time from political figures and business professionals to entertainers. Not only, among the latter, "serious artists and writers" (111) had been increasingly supplanted by individuals associated with the sphere of leisure time, including sports (a category previously absent). More significantly, "the headliners of the movies, the ball parks, and the night clubs" (116) were not described as exemplary characters whose success depended on moral qualities and a good dose of industriousness. In contrast, they appeared as accidental achievers whose stories

DOI: 10.4324/9781003110361-7

retained no teachable or ethical lesson for the public. No longer serving society's primary needs, these selected heroes were "idols of consumption." In Löwenthal's terminology, they had definitively replaced the "idols of production" of the past.

Though seemingly an inconspicuous study of biographies' evolution, Löwenthal's account of the historical apotheosis of a literary genre brilliantly identified the transformative move of American society towards what the historian Warren Susman later defined as the personality culture of the twentieth century—an environment where long-standing qualities previously used to define a person of "character" had been substituted with the flamboyance of "personality" traits.[2] In Susman's assessment, the new figure of the film star epitomized the ascendance of ideals of self-realization in American culture and inevitably obfuscated the previously dominant imperatives of self-sacrifice. As old standards of conduct came to be displaced, a new notion of the self as "performing" began to acquire desirable status, its value based less on achievements than on fame (however generated). Although the United States was still a producer-oriented society, aspirations to celebrity with its emphasis on attractiveness, fandom, and influence engulfed Americans and led them to embrace a fluid sense of worthiness, now redefined in light of novel rules for the presentation of the self. Critically, for our discussion, this emerging stress on a person's mundane charm and performative prowess included the figure of the politician. Although Susman's discussion only alluded to the consequences at the political level of the striving for public admiration in the changed American cultural landscape, the metamorphized role of politicians during the early half of the twentieth century was explicitly illustrated in Löwenthal's study. The content analysis he conducted not only registered a steady decline in the number of biographies dedicated to the political sphere but also identified a simultaneous shift in the content of the profiles of featured politicians. Far from representing examples of professional ethics and dedication, Löwenthal found, politicians were being approached through the petty epics of their private lives in a superficial repetition of facts both obvious and undistinguished. Fully embedded in the culture of personality, politicians were being treated as performers and made to overlap with idols of consumption—a perspective that resonated thousands of miles away from the American coasts. In Italy, Benito Mussolini constituted an early egregious example of the new epochal development that at the dawn of the 1900s had transformed societies' ethical ideals and given rise to the star phenomenon.

There are several reasons for examining Mussolini through the cultural lens of stardom. Both his emergence on the political scene during the 1910s and the eventual construction of his myth as duce of fascism in the 1920s and 1930s benefited from sociocultural changes that promoted the singularity of individual personalities.[3] Also, popular responses to his cult can be elucidated via the link to the nascent phenomenon of consumption as well as the conjuncture of the spectacle of power with the marvel of the show business. But let's proceed in order.

An Early Star

One of the pivotal events that jump-started Mussolini's political career coincided with his intervention at the national congress of the Italian Socialist Party held in Reggio Emilia on July 7, 1912. Almost unknown as a young delegate from the small province of Forlì (he was born in July 1883), Mussolini delivered a speech that attracted the attention of his fellow socialists and ultimately ensured his surprising appointment to the party's national leadership. In truth, behind-the-scenes work allowed Mussolini to push through his agenda and emerge as the vocal representative of the party's revolutionary wing. In other words, his oratorical eloquence alone did not obtain the outcome. Nevertheless, public reactions to his successful participation at the congress doubtlessly showed signs of the emergent cultural tendency (at least in the West) towards privileging seemingly exceptional individuals. Newspaper reports of the event largely focused on the person of Mussolini, whom they saluted as a new figure on the Italian political landscape. Descriptions of him included adjectives such as "crazy, "hotblooded," and "rough," that is, all features that were both unusual and extreme, if not altogether negative, but that nevertheless came to be combined in an overall judgment that emphasized "originality."[4] Standing out, no matter how outrageously, appeared to be the attribute journalists were looking for in a politician. Mussolini fit the ticket perfectly. He was the much sought-after ideal individual expected to shake up an apparently stagnant and spiritually impoverished environment;[5] he was "the man," or a "Man," as some cultural figures began to address him.[6] By the time Mussolini separated from the Socialist Party two years later and founded his own newspaper, he had gained such a renowned reputation that he stood out as one of the most prominent voices for interventionism in World War I (which Italy eventually entered in May 1915).[7] The first, though short, biographical history of Mussolini was published right around this time by his friend Torquato Nanni.[8] Other biographical accounts followed, with a major one by Antonio Beltramelli appearing in 1923, barely a few months after the March on Rome of October 1922.[9] Meanwhile, Mussolini had also written a brief history of his life from birth to November 1911 (which he started in prison in December 1911), as well as a war diary compiled between 1915 and 1917.[10] All these works, which mostly preceded Mussolini's founding of the fascist movement and his eventual ascendance to prime minister of Italy after the staged March on Rome, described him as exceptional and unique—a great personality who was born to be a leader. According to his biographers, a sort of predestination consecrated Mussolini's status as the chosen one, no matter his own developmental trajectory or personal motivations and actions. Nanni portrayed Mussolini as a "spirit of steel"; in turn, Beltramelli, whose book not by chance was titled *The New Man*, called him "the savior."[11] Panegyrics of Mussolini grew exponentially after the king appointed him prime minister at the end of October 1922. By the time Margherita Sarfatti published his first official biography in 1925, Mussolini's destiny as an outstanding figure on the world panorama had been sealed.[12]

In Löwenthal's estimation, biographies and their exponential growth were merely a symptom of cultural shifts. The same goes for the self-help manuals Susman analyzed in his effort to track America's surging interest in personality and the debunking of old-fashioned character. Löwenthal and Susman also agreed that, besides marking a change, printed biographies and personality manuals played a performative role by pushing a new model of personhood that emphasized fame. "*Personality is the quality of being somebody*," the motto went according to Henri Laurent's popular guide.[13] The categories of good and bad having become obsolete, what counted was being famous—an imperative that determined the range of characteristics to be pursued in order to attain celebrity. One had to be "magnetic," "fascinating," "dominant," or merely "extraordinary." Superlatives, Löwenthal indeed found, were now a common stylistic device used by columnists of biographical accounts to describe their heroes. Not surprisingly, Sarfatti's biography of Mussolini highlighted the man's exceptional features and assessed them as an incredible gift of nature. Since childhood, Sarfatti claimed, Mussolini had shown himself to be different—his fate already marked by the higher mandate that would demand he save Italy, "The childhood of superior men is never really happy. . . . The latent forces on a leash within him prevent him from enjoying things quietly like ordinary children."[14] Sarfatti exalted Mussolini's "cursed" uniqueness as a sign of loftiness. Reflecting the trend of other biographies/hagiographies of the fascist leader, she glorified him for defying mortality, as in her description of his "forty-two wounds" in World War I, "He seemed like Saint Sebastian, his flesh pierced as with arrows, scarred in wounds and bathed in blood."[15] Miraculously, Mussolini lived on, his manly strength unmatchable. What more could show his superior status over "mediocre men" than this approximation of sainthood?[16]

In the years leading to Mussolini's meteoric rise to fame, cultural expectations provided the terrain on which the fascist regime eventually deployed political strategies aimed at turning the man into a cult. Mussolini's distinctiveness, whether real or imagined, attracted attention. Once he was appointed prime minister, photographs of Mussolini filled newspapers and periodicals; in turn, the postcard market was flooded with his images. No other Italian politician before him ever experienced such visibility in their institutional role. Magazines' "unpublished photos" of Mussolini came to be advertised as scoops, in an early sign of the paparazzi phenomenon.[17] Explicit references to Mussolini as a personality became the norm. Meanwhile, writings on him multiplied with estimates numbering up to five thousand by 1929.[18] Incidentally, Mussolini's stardom did not merely develop nationally; it found fertile terrain abroad too. Sarfatti's biography was notably published in English first, and many in Europe saluted Mussolini's rise as a welcome sign of Italy's regeneration. In the United States, popular weeklies and monthly magazines hailed Mussolini's threatened coup d'état after the March on Rome—a preview of the myth of "the right dictator" that circulated after Mussolini's authoritarian turn in 1925.[19] Even Mussolini's *My Autobiography* published in the United States in 1928 might have been authored by the former American ambassador in Italy, Richard Washburn Child, a Harvard Law graduate that upon returning from Italy in 1924 became editor of *The Saturday Evening Post*. In his official foreword to the volume, Child referred to Mussolini's government as "superstatesmanship."[20] The ex-ambassador enthusiastically emphasized that Mussolini had made a state—not a small feat by any measure. Positive evaluations of Mussolini in the United States seemed taken out of the best early-twentieth-century self-help manuals on personality: he was "forceful," "attractive," "magnetic," "energetic," in one word, "extraordinary."[21] Following a similarly hyperbolic approach, this is how the man himself (or his ghost writers) recounted his wounding in World War I in *My Autobiography*, "I faced atrocious pain; my suffering was indescribable. I underwent practically all my operations without the aid of an anaesthetic. I had twenty-seven operations in one month; all but two were without anaesthetics."[22]

It soon appeared evident to many that, similarly to a commodity, Mussolini sold, whether it was his images, words, or paraphernalia. Stores even featured soap bars in the shape of the dictator, as the French journalist Henri Béraud marveled during a visit to Italy in 1929.[23] By this time, of course, the official construction of the myth of Mussolini had begun in earnest. A whole propaganda apparatus was set up by the regime to orchestrate campaigns and ensure the magnification of the duce in what had become a de facto one-party state. This organization of Mussolini's myth was facilitated by the celebrity aura that since early in his political career had created a star out of an enterprising, and obviously astute, young politician. Mussolini took advantage of the hunger for novelty voiced by many intellectuals and cultural critics throughout the first decades of the twentieth century. On that ground, he was able to recruit adepts and eventually build a relationship between himself as the leader and the Italians as his followers. This bond was based on an implicit understanding that the success of personalities depended on the attraction they exercised over the mass of "mediocre" admirers. Indeed, one cannot understand the myth of Mussolini without taking into account the role of its interlocutors in a symbiotic union that, though characterized by the dominance of the leader, at the same time showed the leader's dependency on the "crowd" that sustained him.

The Leader and the Masses

According to both Löwenthal and Susman, biographies and self-help manuals magnified ordinary people's deficiencies and touted the supposed distance separating the exceptional man from the masses. They did so, however, through a series of paradoxes. On the one hand, in an environment that tended to present any merchandise in inflated terms by transforming "the average into the extraordinary," the uniqueness of advertised commodities applied to anything and anybody, from toothpastes to sportsmen, leading to a sort of normalization of exceptionality.[24] At the same time, because the language of promotion replaced the language of evaluation, readers/admirers were left with no roadmaps for emulating their heroes, further deepening their sense of littleness and their susceptibility to the influence of the great man—one's everyday life still appeared insignificant when compared to the hyped success of entertainment figures. On the other hand, idols of consumption could not survive without people's interest in them. Celebrities had to appeal to the average person and pretend to engage with them, rather than choosing to withdraw to the ivory tower of their presumed superiority. Their life was supposed to be an open book (as far as that went in these popular biographies), and readers were made to experience an exclusive access to their heroes, though of course exclusivity was ironically extended to the millions. In sum, popularity was rooted on people's support and, most importantly, depended on gratifying their curiosity. Self-help manuals pushed the imperative of likeability especially far. As Orison Swett Marden advised in his *Masterful Personality*, "You can compel people to like you," a suggestion that doubtlessly encouraged fake behavior and artificiality, and pretense too. One needed "to know what to say and how to say it," Marden's manual insisted. In addition, and closely linked to that advice, personalities had to accept the limits of their adoring publics and feel a close attachment to them, "You must like other people and not be resentful."[25] Simulation, dependency, and likeability were intricately entwined as personalities needed to bond with their "inferior" admirers.

Though neither Laurent nor Marden mentioned Gustave Le Bon in their popular treatises, his *La psychologie des foules* (1895) had been a trend setter in the new "science" of subtle manipulation that flourished at the turn of the century. Le Bon's suggestions were particularly directed at political leaders,

> When crowds have come . . . to acquire a profound antipathy for the images evoked by certain words, the first duty of the statesman is to change words without, of course, laying hands on the things themselves, the latter being too intimately bound up with the inherited constitution to be transformed. . . . The power of words is so great that it suffices to designate in well-chosen terms the most odious things to make them acceptable to crowds.

Driven by a deep scorn for the masses, Le Bon proposed that to engage the multitudes one needed to appeal to their sentiments and "pretend to share these sentiments."[26] Incidentally, Le Bon became Mussolini's self-declared mentor in the art of persuasion.[27]

Obviously, a double bind tied the "exceptional" figures who had been able to emerge out of the crowd to those who failed to stand out from the midst.

As the same Mussolini recognized in the preface to the English version of Sarfatti's biography, the power of attraction exerted by remarkable individuals was by no means unilateral, absolute, or unidirectional,

> I have sometimes meditated upon the fate, grotesque and sublime, of the public man. But I have not arrived at any conclusions, just because it is Fate we have to deal with. The public man is born 'public'—he bears the stigma from his birth. . . . I am perfectly resigned to my lot as a public man. In fact, I am enthusiastic about it . . . it is the thought, the realization, that I no longer belong merely to myself, that I belong to all—loved by all, hated by all—that I am an essential element in the lives of others: this feeling has on me a kind of intoxicating effect.[28]

With impressive precision, Mussolini's romanticized approach to his own fame captured the leader's dependency on the masses and their mood, a mood that needed to be cultivated and groomed in order eventually to control it. The leader, Mussolini also publicly acknowledged in a 1921 speech, ought to overcome feelings of superiority and scorn, "In me two Mussolinis fight: one who is individualist and does not love the masses, the other absolutely disciplined."[29] Sarfatti's biography echoed that statement, "But how could he love humans? He sees them as they are with pitiless clairvoyance."[30] Mussolini loving humans? What an absurd demand, Sarfatti hinted. His superior and extraordinary status was above the common person's condition, and a hiatus separated him from the masses as a god from humans. And yet, although Mussolini approximated a deity, reality dictated that he wins the masses over, for his existence depended on them. Mussolini's exceptionality could only be proven via a comparison that brought to the open the mediocre status of those surrounding him and that he so much despised,

> When I feel the masses in my hands, since they believe in me, or when I mingle with them, and they almost crush me, then I feel like one with the masses. However, there is at the same time a little aversion, much as the poet feels towards the material he works with.[31]

Totally identifying with his role of exceptional leader, Mussolini struggled to descend from the height of his grander status to confront the ordinariness of the average person. Facing this predicament, he certainly felt victim of an unfair exchange, since the Italians, as it turns out, were not quite bending to his aesthetic vision. Their raw material, he will disconsolately declare at the end of his dictatorship, was not of the quality needed for a work of art.

In truth, and Mussolini's self-pity aside, the Italian "masses" were dealt a worse hand than him in this turbulent romance. As the recipients of Mussolini's grace, all they could do was worship and be in awe of such a loftier being and feel lucky to be led by him. They were expected to consume mentally and materially the image of this mythical man, vicariously bask in his glory, and accept their passive role in the relationship. The omnipresence of Mussolini facilitated this inequitable arrangement, even though it simultaneously made possible the public's admission into the dream world of celebrities. The new means of communication, in particular, allowed Italians to feel proximity to the dictator when not able to witness him in person during official rallies and celebrations. The radio, as well as the moving images in the form of newsreels, gave spectators an almost unlimited access to Mussolini and his actions, family life, thoughts, and mind. Mussolini indeed belonged to all, as he surmised, though of course all belonged to him. That is how the game of personality worked. And it required continuous feeding and upkeep. Taking into account that Mussolini's leadership of Italy lasted over twenty years, the plethora of representations that circulated about him during the regime worked to keep alive his myth. From the reassuring and hardworking image of the farmer to the daring figure of the aviator, Mussolini offered a variety of attractive solicitations to one's fantasy world; he satisfied many a taste. Not only a person of culture and vast knowledge for some, embracer of modern creations such as cars and motorbikes for others, but also a reassuring family man, respected stateman, and even conqueror of colonies and founder of a new empire in 1936—the dynamic variety of roles Mussolini played contributed to foster his fame and increase his attraction. In the prevailing culture of consumption, he competed with the idols of Hollywood and dominated the market. Like movie stars, he made his followers dream, though in his case by soliciting nationalistic and imperialistic aspirations. Better than the movie stars, however, he realized those dreams no matter how perversely pursued. Poisoning and massacring his way through Ethiopia, in 1936, he enacted Italy's much sought-after empire and succeeded in propagating the illusion of strength in a country soon to experience an economic crisis of catastrophic proportions.

The myth of Mussolini lived on even as autarchy became more of a necessity than a choice and as the regime's delusions of grandeur reached absurd heights via unreasonable demands on the most intimate aspects of Italians' daily lives. The belief in Mussolini's greatness and purposefulness was hard to dismantle despite his disastrous decision on June 10, 1940, to lead the country into World War II. When Mussolini was deposed and arrested in July 1943, following the negative vote of members of his Grand Council, Italy had been waging war for three years. In the following twenty-two months, the country would be subjected to a devastating German occupation, endless deadly bombings by Allied forces, and a civil war. To be sure, the population rejoiced at the fall of fascism in July 1943. However, whereas popular manifestations of relief were particularly directed at the destruction of Mussolini's images, many Italians believed that he had made mistakes but was not solely guilty. Instead, the fascist experiment was botched by those around the dictator who profited from their position of power while promoting malfeasance and corruption.[32] Only once the brutish reality of war and occupation worsened did the Italians' rejection of Mussolini deepen. Particularly jarring in the eyes of the people was the execution of Mussolini's son-in-law carried out under the auspices of the new republican government set up by Mussolini in northern Italy with the assistance of Hitler's armies. Galeazzo Ciano, husband of his "favorite" child Edda, was put on trial and sentenced to death in January 1944 for the role he played in the July 1943 fall of his father-in-law. Not even a daughter's pleas persuaded Mussolini to reverse course. Among the many terrible acts committed by the fascists, this vengeful miscarriage of justice curiously struck Italians and more than other deeds exposed to them the tyrannical nature of the past regime. An internecine family blood bath, which dramatically refracted the fratricidal war pitting Italian against Italian, became the utmost crime of a weakened leader who could not accept the fact that his end had come.

The Leader and the Masses II: Trump, Minus the Macabre of Family Drama

Fast-forward to the late twentieth and beginning of the twenty-first centuries, the stars of the marquee (originally the matrix for idols of consumption) enter the world of public affairs. Instead of political figures being treated as celebrities, the opposite trend unfolds: movie stars turn into politicians. Ronald Reagan and Arnold Schwarzenegger rose through their party's ranks and assumed the presidency of the country and the governorship of California, respectively, qua representatives of the Hollywood industry. Then, in 2015, another mutation transpired in the twisted relation between fame and politics. Candidate Donald Trump, whose notoriety was built on aggrandized business credentials and a popular reality TV show, exemplified the power of generic, empty celebrity as guarantee for accessing the supposedly serious realm of governing. Not even an acting career was required any longer. Coming full circle, the dilution of the value of expertise and solid competency reached total liquefaction—perhaps another sign (both metaphorical and factual) of what the sociologist Zygmunt Bauman defines as liquid modernity.

To the value of character already dismissed a century earlier, Trump's candidacy added the possession of credentials as cause for disqualification from serving in the highest office. Claims of bravura, however false, became a sufficient reason for eligibility and an effective lure for electors tired of politics as usual. Building on an infamous work of ghost writing (*Trump: The Art of the Deal*), Trump's fame had risen from tabloid exploits and gossip magazines' columns to a semi-serious consideration of his presumed business abilities. A "nonfiction work of fiction," as one journalist defined it,[33] *The Art of the Deal* was inspired by a cover story on Trump published in the May 1984 issue of the magazine for men GQ dedicated to the theme, "Success: How Sweet It Is: Men Who Take Risks and

Make Millions." The feature article took Trump as a paragon of success intended in the crudest sense of one's ability to make money, purely and simply.[34] In spite of a glamorous description of Trump's trophies, including material and human properties (his wife and football team among others), the article appeared to suggest between the lines that the man from Queens was unfittingly and maladroitly invading Manhattan's superior culture, the gaudiness of his cuffs a conspicuous sign of his "provincial" or parvenu status.[35] Not by any stretch a member of the selected few that formed the aristocracy of real Manhattanites, Trump was on a crusade to humiliate the "elites" with flashy enterprises, the exact signal of his failure to join their circle. The splashiness of (big) size, it turns out, was already an obsession of his, and he obviously took it as the only attribute that could differentiate him from the established refinement of old-money wealth.[36] Embracing his own crassness, Trump gloated in his barbarian invading tactics, knowing very well that the brashness of a salesman was his strongest asset. "And if there's a reason I'm good promotionally, it's that I know what people want," the article quoted him. Meeting people's expectations was high on his list of strategies for success—an advice that self-help manuals on personality had begun to dispense earlier on in the century.

As usual, publicity generated more publicity. The issue of the GQ magazine featuring Trump sold surprisingly well, and there followed the proposal for a book that would lay out Trump's deal-making rules—a golden idea.[37] Launched with a glitzy publicity campaign, including a Trump-style party and media appearances, *Trump: The Art of the Deal* was published in 1987, soon to become a best seller. Aside from the usual aggrandizement typical of biographies, the book contained an 11-step blueprint for success in business, which reinforced the claim, whether real or fictional, that Trump possessed a winning formula. Propped by this claim to fame, Trump published more advice manuals on entrepreneurship, wealth, and even golfing. Then, in 2004, he was offered a protagonist role in the reality TV show *The Apprentice*, a chance that definitively expanded the range and number of people familiar with his name. Previously, he had appeared throughout the 1990s as a regular guest on the *Howard Stern Show*. Later, in 2011, he began a weekly commentary on *Fox and Friends*, adding one building block of public exposure to another. By the time he launched his own political campaign in the American presidential election of 2016, after an initial exploratory attempt in 2000, Trump's popularity had grown exponentially. Although it is hard to establish whether business credentials or the success he found as a television celebrity boosted his likeability scores, we know for certain that Trump relied on Nielsen ratings to measure his newfound fame as a performer. Having achieved high visibility, he identified a political path for himself while turning lack of expertise and competence into keys for holding office. Paradoxically, many Americans seemingly dissatisfied with governing figures believed that playing politician (through, literally, impersonation and imposture) might lead to mending the ills of government.

From the start, Trump's political venture was entangled with his business and entertainment life, while Twitter became a cipher of his cunning use of means of communication.[38] All the ostentatiousness of his past attempts at making it in the exclusive club of Manhattanites continued to be a feature of his political ambitions. Even more significant, his daring attempt to hold public office confirmed the importance he assigned to a critical element for success: personal triumph depended on interpreting people's desires. And this rule applied no matter who his interlocutors were. Rumor goes that at first Trump reacted negatively to the proposal of playing host on *The Apprentice*. The whole genre of reality TV appeared to him as geared "for the bottom-feeders of society," a category of people he was obviously not keen at being associated with.[39] Many seasons later, those "bottom-feeders" made his ascent to political leadership a reality. The popularity they ensured Trump during the successful run of the show and afterwards became the knot linking Trump ever so tightly to them, a knot he was never able to untie and almost fatalistically came to accept. President Trump's fixation with polls, which logically followed his original focus on promotion, implied that he ought to give the people what they wanted. Although he was ominously right in predicting that he could shoot somebody on Fifth Avenue and get away with it (as his multiple unpunished crimes testify), his status as chained to his followers' opinions paradoxically held. In the tradition of the American demagogue, Trump used techniques of agitation as "means of antidemocratic manipulation."[40] If he was supposed to feed his admirers fabricated stories that would show his upper hand in the relationship, however, he failed. When faced with a situation of public health crisis that could have showcased his leadership had he taken the right actions, he opted not to alarm people. He feared their reactions. As he obliviously told Bob Woodward apropos Covid-19, "I wanted to always play it down. I still like playing it down because I don't want to create a panic."[41] Screaming delirium of omnipotence from all his pores, Trump appeared in charge of the narrative he spun and yet fell victim to the power of his audience all the same. He conceded to what he believed were his admirers' expectations, indirectly admitting he could not steer them in whichever direction he decided—he was not able to maintain his edge. The masqueraded, rowdy crowd that stormed the capital on January 6, 2021, might be the lasting image of Trump's inevitable dependency on those bottom-feeders he admittedly despised. His aspiration to join the circle of the select few of moneyed Manhattanites was definitively crushed by the violent image of a crashing mob whose members turned out to be the only ones unconditionally accepting him in their midst. With ominous parallels to Mussolini's story, Trump's son-in-law might be the biggest beneficiary of the tycoon-turned-president's tumble. Denied a second term, and his autocratic dreams rebuffed, Trump was spared the potential scenario as befallen to Mussolini of having to sacrifice a favorite daughter's sentiments in the vain attempt to remain in power—a macabre family drama that never was and, hopefully, never will be.

Notes

1 See Leo Löwenthal, *Literature, Popular Culture, and Society* (Palo Alto: Pacific Books, 1961), 109–140. The chapter was first published as "Biographies in Popular Magazines," in Paul Lazarsfeld and Frank Stanton (eds.), *Radio Research: 1942–1943* (New York: Duell, Sloan and Pearce, 1944).
2 Warren Susman, "'Personality' and Twentieth-Century Culture," in *Culture as History: The Transformation of American Society in the Twentieth Century* (New York: Pantheon Books, 1973), 271–285.
3 Simonetta Falasca-Zamponi, "The Culture of Personality: Mussolini and the Cinematic Imagination," in Klaus Heller and Jan Plamper (eds.), *Personality Cults in Stalinism* (Göttingen: V & R Unipress, 2004).
4 Simonetta Falasca-Zamponi, *Fascist Spectacle: The Aesthetics of Power in Mussolini's Italy* (Berkeley: University of California Press, 1997).
5 I'm not implying that his speech was merely full of empty words. Its content was certainly appealing due to an emphasis on spiritual values and a denunciatory attack of old-style politics. Mussolini also pitted revolutionary socialism against the reformist wing of the party.
6 Falasca-Zamponi, *Fascist Spectacle*, 43–44.
7 This went against the socialists' position of neutrality.
8 Torquato Nanni, *Benito Mussolini* (Florence: Libreria della Voce, 1915) reprinted in Emilio Gentile ed., *Mussolini e "La Voce"* (Florence: Sansoni, 1976).
9 Antonio Beltramelli, *L'Uomo nuovo* (Milan: Mondadori, 1923).
10 Benito Mussolini, "La mia vita dal 29 luglio 1883 al 23 novembre 1911" and "Il mio diario di guerra," in *Opera Omnia* (Florence: La Fenice, 1951–1963), vols. XXXIII and XXXIV.
11 Other biographies emphasizing the idea of Mussolini's novelty along similar lines were Guglielmo Policastro, *Homus novus* (The new man) (Catania: Minerva, 1923) and Omero Petri, *L'italiano nuovissimo (il Messia)* (The Very New Italian, the Messiah) (Turin: Bocca, 1928).
12 Margherita Sarfatti, *The Life of Benito Mussolini* (London: Thornton Butterworth, 1925). The Italian version was published a year later as *Dux* (Milan: Mondadori, 1926). Biographies were scarce in Italy. This makes the high volume of biographies covering Mussolini even more relevant.
13 Henri Laurent, *Personality: How to Build It* (New York and London: Funk & Wagnalls Company, 1915), 25 (in italics in the original), first published in French in 1914 as *La personnalité*.
14 Sarfatti, *The Life of Benito Mussolini*, 37.
15 Ibid., 230.
16 In the Italian 1934 version of the preceding quote, Sarfatti wrote, "The children who are predestined to great things ignore the natural and pleasant equilibrium of mediocre men." See *Dux* (Milan: Mondadori, 1934). The English and Italian versions of Sarfatti's biography are different, as are the several Italian editions.
17 *Illustrazione Italiana*, 13 April 1924.
18 Dino Biondi, *La fabbrica del Duce* (Florence: Vallecchi, 1967).
19 John Diggins, *Mussolini and Fascism: The View from America* (Princeton: Princeton University Press, 1972).
20 Benito Mussolini, *My Autobiography* (New York: Charles Scribner's Sons, 1928), with a Foreword by Richard Washburn Child, p. xi. It is believed that the ambassador wrote the book in collaboration with Mussolini's brother, Arnaldo.

21 On the United States' love affair with Mussolini, see John Diggins.
22 *My Autobiography*, 48. This is the same episode cited by Sarfatti through the evocation of Saint Sebastian.
23 *Ce que j'ai vu à Rome* (Paris: Les Editions de France, 1929). Béraud's account described the several signs of Mussolini's omnipresence in the country.
24 Löwenthal, *Literature, Popular Culture, and Society*, 130.
25 Orison Swett Marden, *Masterful Personality* (New York: Thomas Y. Crowell Company, 1921), 279.
26 *The Crowd: A Study of the Popular Mind* (New York: Viking, 1960), 106–107, 113.
27 Mussolini's interview with the Paris review *La science et la vie* of June 1926 in *Opera Omnia*, vol. XXII, p. 156
28 Sarfatti, *Dux*, 9–10.
29 The speech was delivered at the Fascist Party Congress on November 7, 1921, now in *Scritti e discorsi* (Milan: Hoepli, 1934–1939), vol. II, p. 205.
30 Sarfatti, *Dux*, 313.
31 Ludwig, *Colloqui con Mussolini* (Milan: Mondadori, 1932), 125.
32 Simonetta Falasca-Zamponi, "Ordinary Antifascism? Italy and the Fall of Fascism, 1943–1945," *Journal of Modern Italian Studies*, vol. 24, no. 1 (2019), 171–189.
33 Timothy O'Brien as cited by Jane Mayer, "Donald Trump's Ghostwriter Tells All," *The New Yorker*, 25 July 2016.
34 The article in GQ "Donald Trump Gets What He Wants" was written by Graydon Carter.
35 "About the only thing that gives away this striver from an outer borough are his cuff links: huge mollusks of gold and stone the size of half-dollars." "The hands small" were also noted at this time. Ibid.
36 In another notable line, Carter stated, "Double-parked outside is a half-block-long Cadillac stretch limo with 'DJT' vanity plate." He also added that Trump was "plastering the family name on any blank surface that rose and shined." Ibid.
37 In the article, Carter wrote, "As in the movies, success in real estate often depends on the deal, and Trump, in his relatively short career, has proved himself a remarkably deft dealmaker."
38 *The Apprentice* was recorded in a special set created in Trump Tower. Trump could leave his business office on the upper floors and perform in the show before going back up to his more serious affairs. Later, the set of *The Apprentice* became the headquarters of his presidential campaign.
39 Cited among others by Michael Kranish, "A Fierce Will to Win Pushed Donald Trump to the Top," *Washington Post*, 20 June 2017.
40 For an instructive analysis of the effects of political "agitators" on their audiences see Leo Löwenthal and Norbert Guterman, *Prophets of Deceit: A Study of the Techniques of the American Agitator* (New York: Harper, 1949). In his introduction to the volume, Max Horkheimer wrote, "Our homegrown agitators, in the absence of an American tradition of nationalistic aggressiveness, created an artificial fusion with Italian and German fascist notions. They have also borrowed from certain forms of religious revivalism," xii. The agitator's playbook as spelled out in *Prophets of Deceit* rings eerily current with Trump and the conspiratorial right.
41 From transcript of phone call with Bob Woodward (February 7, 2020).

8

DONALD TRUMP, MAO ZEDONG AND RELIGIOUS ANTI-INTELLECTUALISM

Bin Song

> "So, what did Jesus think of the Pharisees?" . . . "You guys are hypocrites because you make sure that your words are right, but you don't do a thing about it." So, I tried to think, "Well, how is that in our day?" Well, it's like having the right doctrinal statement, making sure it is known that you have the right doctrinal statement. In fact, you will do everything to make sure that people see it. You know, you put it on the Web, you put it in a nice booklet, you get the precise wording, you have the right proof texts. You're meticulous about everything, even maybe the right format, even the right font. Okay, because this is important, right? But it's all done for show. When it comes to doing the statement, well, what you start to get is, "We'll get around to it, eventually. But we've got a good one."
>
> —*Pastor Lonnie, sermon on Mark 7:13 delivered at Riverside Bible Church, U.S., in March of 2016*[1]

> The door of sagely learning was blocked, and it was no longer to be seen. Therefore the learning of textual criticism developed and those perpetuating it were regarded as famous. The practice of memorization and recitation developed and those advocating it were regarded as extensively learned. The writing of flowery compositions developed and those indulging in it were regarded as elegant. Thus with great confusion and tremendous noise they set themselves up and competed with one another, and no one knew how many schools there were. Among tens of thousands of paths and thousands of tracks, none knew which to follow. . . . Extensive memorization and recitation merely served to increase scholar's pride, substantial and abundant knowledge merely served to help them to do evil, enormous information merely served to help them

DOI: 10.4324/9781003110361-8

> indulge in argumentation, and wealth in flowery compositions merely served to cover up their hypocrisy.
>
> —*Wang Yangming (1472–1529), "Pulling Up the Root and Stopping Up the Source," written in Ming Dynasty of China in 1525*[2]

It may not be conventional to start a chapter with two long epigraphs, especially when considering the fact that the statuses of the two quoted authors in their respective traditions are barely comparable to each other. Pastor Lonnie ministers an evangelical family church located in a midsized city of the southwestern United States, with about 140 weekly attendees who are predominantly white and middle-aged, including many retirees.[3] In contrast, Wang Yangming is widely considered as one most significant Ru[4] thinker, the influence of whom in the late imperial and early modern periods of the Ru tradition in East Asia may be secondary only to his rivaling predecessor, Zhu Xi (1130–1200).

Nevertheless, it is no longer a secret that evangelical Christians furnished the strongest religious support of the Trump presidency. It is also recognized that the key message delivered by Pastor Lonnie shares a general anti-intellectual mentality among nationwide evangelical Christians in the United States.[5] Similarly, despite the fact that followers of Wang Yangming and Zhu Xi continually debated upon the role of empirical knowledge in moral self-cultivation, Wang's moral philosophy with its latent anti-intellectualism had become a triumphant voice resonated among enthusiastic reformers and revolutionaries who strived for saving China from her national crises triggered by the invasion of the colonial West since 1840s.[6]

It is the comparable impact of "religious anti-intellectualism" of the named two traditions, viz., evangelical Christianity and the Wang Yangming school of heartmind[7] (心學, xinxue) of Ruism, upon, respectively, the Trump presidency and the reign of Mao Zedong over the People's Republic of China (PRC) which justifies my juxtaposing the two epigraphs. In this chapter, I will seek to argue several major points to demonstrate the reign of Mao Zedong as a precedent of the Trump presidency.

Firstly, both the Trump presidency and the Mao reign are characterized by anti-intellectualism, and a religious dimension registers in each anti-intellectualism.

Secondly, the religious dimension of Trumpist anti-intellectualism lies in how evangelical Christians pit "heart knowledge" against "head knowledge" via a specific type of biblical hermeneutics. The one of Maoist anti-intellectualism is historically rooted in how Wang Yangming and his followers advocated the superior role of "attaining conscientious awareness" (致良知, zhiliangzhi) over the pursuit of empirical knowledge in an individual's moral self-cultivation.

Thirdly, to prohibit the undesirable impact of such religious anti-intellectualisms upon public life, affiliates and sympathizers with each tradition need to utilize their own traditional sources to reconsider the relationship between faith and reason, or the relationship between a religious practitioner's ultimate concern and preliminary concerns.

Trumpist Anti-Intellectualism and Its Religious Dimension

Since Richard Hofstadter's *Anti-Intellectualism in American Life* (1963), scholars have defined "anti-intellectualism" varyingly.[8] Because I'll compare the religious dimensions of anti-intellectualism in two different cases, my definition, while informed by others, is intended to highlight the common feature of both: anti-intellectualism is a resentment and suspicion towards the value of empirical knowledge which is produced by intellectual elite via the method of rational criticism.

In light of the increasingly polarized American politics, Scholars also analyzed varying dimensions of American anti-intellectualism, as well as manifestations of the anti-intellectualism among evangelical voters. Because of the following reasons, the Trump presidency can be seen as having intensely manifested all major dimensions of American anti-intellectualism: anti-rationalist, anti-elitist and instrumentalist.[9] Firstly, as being supported strongly by evangelical voters, the Trumpist anti-intellectualism had a conspicuous religious implication, which is anti-rationalist and will be analyzed thematically later. Secondly, there was a rhetorical pattern of Trump's speeches which pitted "the people" against the established class of intellectual and social elite. The incited hostility inhibited the implementation of progressive policies normally supported by American intellectual elite, such as eradication of poverty, healthcare reform, climate change legislation, and social restrictions during the Covid-19 pandemic.[10] Thirdly, as frequently touting himself as a business genius whose career had been deliberately detached from politics, Trump's election amplified the instrumentalist suspicion among American capitalists towards the value of higher education which takes the creation of well-rounded scientists, experts, and rigorously scrutinized empirical knowledge as a major task.

Clearly, the religious support furnished by evangelical voters is just one among many reasons why anti-intellectualism prevailed under the aegis of the Trump presidency. However, as stated by the National Association of Evangelicals in an article calling evangelicals to action: "never before has God given American Evangelicals such an awesome opportunity to shape public policy in ways that could contribute to the well-being of the entire world,"[11] the anti-intellectual character of evangelical Christianity is capable of generating significant impact in real politics if under certain circumstances (such as the Trump presidency), objective conditions converge into a favorable environment for the wide spread of anti-intellectualism in society.

Be that as it may, it is all too obvious that not all Christians look like the majority of evangelicals towards and during the Trump presidency. In other words, the marriage of anti-intellectualism with Christianity requires a specific type of biblical hermeneutics, as well as an accompanying mindset or strategy to perpetuate the hermeneutics in real politics. In the following, I'll analyze the evangelical biblical hermeneutics to compare it later with the religious dimension of Maoist anti-intellectualism.

An evident reason for evangelicals to remain suspicious towards the intellect lies in their fear that intellectualism calls their faith into doubt and leads to adopting science, secularism, and relativism.[12] However, the tension of faith and reason has been rooted in the West ever since the convergence of ancient Greek philosophies and Christianity in the late antique Europe. Given abundant variations of the way how Christian denominations and thinkers have addressed the tension, it is not necessary that such a tension develops into a full-fledged anti-intellectualism. Therefore, we need concrete analyses to set light upon how the evangelical reading of the Bible leads to anti-intellectualism.

Fortunately, Mark Ward Sr.'s field study on the sermons of Pastor Lonnie furnishes such a concrete case. While analyzing the biblical hermeneutics in Pastor Lonnie's sermons, Ward comments:

> Evangelicals believe that the scriptures are inspired by God and provide believers an inerrant "manual for living." Thus, the chief aim of evangelical Bible study is making *applications* to personal concerns of the moment. So long as chapter and verse are cited, applications are seen as valid appropriations of biblical authority. Nor are applications constrained by the original historical meaning intended by the author since the Bible is viewed as God's Word for all times and all cultures. Taking the Bible literally thus equates to a plain reading of the text; inquiring into its literary provenance or structure, on the other hand, would hinder its accessibility and relevance.
>
> Because the Bible is regarded by evangelicals as self-authenticating and thus *the best interpreter of itself*, teaching and preaching typically devolve either into narrative preaching that cites a proof text and then illustrates it through a series of stories, or into expository preaching that often relies on *word studies* or picking out keywords in the text and then reciting other Bible verses where the same word appears. . . . congregational norms are created not only, or even primarily, by the *content* of what the leaders said but, rather, the construction of identities and social structures . . . are profoundly shaped by the *form* of suasion that a given leader normalizes.[13]

Given such a way of reading the Christian Bible, it is no wonder that Pastor Lonnie, in the quoted epigraph, can liken "Pharisees" to scientists, experts, and even sophisticated biblical scholars who do care about the literary provenance or structure of biblical verses. Hence, Pastor Lonnie is also able to deliver anti-intellectual weekly sermons to construct a strong evangelical identity for the local Riverside Bible Church. Several major points of this evangelical biblical hermeneutics are summarized as follows:

1 The Bible is inerrant and needs to be read plainly.
2 It is individuals who, in reliance upon their religious devotion rather than discursive intellect, hold onto the final authority of reading the Bible plainly.
3 The value of the devotional reading of biblical verses consists in how to apply them to address personal concerns of the moment.

There is a discernable superiority of action and emotion over intellect in the hermeneutics, which illuminates evangelical Christianity as a hotbed of political movements featured by anti-intellectualism such as the Trump presidency. More importantly, pivoting upon contextless reading and personal application to daily life, the hermeneutics speaks to the overall nature of evangelical politics. It has been noticed that there is no evangelical system of social thought, and hence, "many evangelicals seem to find their theory merely by following the contours of the political movement that is currently defending, and exploiting them."[14] In other words, the political engagement of evangelicals is more reactionary to situational opponents, rather than proactive out of well-articulated and systemized moral principles. This is the reason why they do not only support political campaigns per their adjudication of wedge issues such as gay marriage and abortion which seem to be of biblical relevance. Evangelicals also espouse conservative political agendas that, without apparent biblical references, happen to belong to political movements which currently employ the evangelical constituency.

A few examples would suffice to demonstrate how the Trump presidency tapped into the anti-intellectual mentality of evangelical Christianity shaped by such biblical hermeneutics and, hence, has become the most prominent force of evangelical politics so far. On the level of policy making, it is well documented that the Trump presidency and its conservative political allies overtly utilized the evangelically manufactured antagonism of faith versus reason to justify policies contrary to the consensus of scientists and experts, such as rolling back environmental protection[15] and defying social restrictions during the Covid-19 pandemic.[16] Moreover, despite his apparent lack of religious education in the Bible,[17] when Trump personally cited the scripture in speeches, his offhand usage of biblical tropes often reminds us of how Pastor Lonnie read the Bible "plainly" in order to address personal concerns of the moment, albeit Trump's usage on a politically much more potent scale. For instance, Trump said he was "the chosen one" for "taking on China on trade," and he also endorsed the idea propagated by a conservative radio host that in light of Trump's foreign policy, Israeli Jews see him as the "second coming of God."[18] Regarding such egregious usage of the Bible in real politics, I believe no scenario is more defining the Trump presidency than on June 1, 2020, when a peaceful crowd of

George Floyd protesters were forcefully cleared from Lafayette Square to create a path for President Trump to walk from the White House to the St. John's Episcopal Church. Trump then held up a Bible and posed for a photo op in front of the church's parish house. Remarkable points of this religious and political stunt include: firstly, the held Bible was admitted by Trump as not his own; secondly, the Episcopal Church neither invited Trump nor identifies itself among evangelical Christians.[19] Regardless of these contextless ways of employing the Bible, what Trump actually accomplished was to claim a biblical authority via a photo op for his highly divisive political response to the protest and hence exploit the ethos of Christian nationalism among white evangelical Christians for partisan political purposes. Emphatically, employing while exploiting, such a manipulative use of the Bible has epitomized the definitive feature of evangelical politics analyzed earlier.

Maoist Anti-Intellectualism and Its Religious Foundation

Perceptive scholars in the United States have noticed the similarity between Mao Zedong and American populist politicians such as Donald Trump and Andrew Jackson. For instance, Melissa Macauley opines in *Washington Post*:

> There are many differences between Mao and Trump, but their similarities are uncanny. Both are sons of wealthy landlords. Both rely on ties to propaganda machines to stoke hatred of ostensible enemies. Both sabotage international alliances. The political rallies of both men are vermilion spectacles of adulation as the legions hold aloft their 'Little Red Books' or adorn their crowns with red MAGA caps. Such populist extravaganzas manifest their unparalleled political advantages.[20]

However, concerning the topic of this chapter, there are abundant evidences of anti-intellectualism especially towards the last decade of Mao's reign, viz., the Cultural Revolution. In one noticeable occasion that reminds of Trump's claim "I don't think science knows" to deny the impact of climate change on California's wildfires in 2020,[21] Mao Zedong pronounced the demerit of critically minded intellectuals in 1966 as follows:

> Those professors and students in college can only bite their books (which is an easier job to do): firstly, they cannot fight a war; secondly, they cannot contribute to revolution; thirdly, they cannot do factory work; fourthly, they cannot plow any field. Their knowledge is extremely poor, and they know nothing about these mentioned jobs. As always, some of them do have knowledge on one topic, which is to counter communism, the people, and revolution. They also have a "method" which is the one of countering revolution. Therefore, I usually say that compared with

> factory workers and peasants, intellectuals are the least knowledgeable. They never feel a regret when they toil from one book to another, and from one concept to another. If they continue to do, they cannot do anything other than countering revolution, reviving capitalism, and developing revisionism.[22]

These words indicate that the Maoist anti-intellectualism has its strong anti-elitist and instrumentalist connotations. However, it is replete with anti-rationalism as well. During the tumultuous decade of Cultural Revolution, Mao believed that the key factor for the desired social transformation of China to communism is not objective reality (traditionally considered by Marxists as necessary for any change of social superstructure) but the knowledge and will of each individual. Such a Maoist voluntarism[23] does not only project a perfect future as the end of human history that can be finally and fully realized and hence is utopian in nature. But it also asserts that China can reply upon the correct knowledge and will of each individual. And this can be achieved mainly through ideological inculcation and organized mass movements. In a word, the Maoist voluntarism pits the will of the people with the critical rationality of intellectual elite and hence entails the anti-rationalist nature of Maoist anti-intellectualism.

Nevertheless, in contrast with the case of the Trumpist anti-intellectualism which has a conspicuous religious dimension illustrated earlier, it remains a controversy among scholars whether there is any religious characteristic of the Maoist anti-intellectualism. When the Cultural Revolution started to be reported in the West, scholars readily recognized the phenomenon of Maoism as a "quasi-religion."[24] The current scholarship also focuses upon Maoism as a "political religion," via methods such as tracing the historical development of such a religion to its earlier Yanan period or indicating the similarity of it with other Western totalitarian political movements in the 20th century.[25] Be that as it may, it is the character traits of Mao and the sociological features of the political movement under the banner of Maoism which have intrigued these scholars to portray Maoism as being religious. While doing so, scholars liken those character traits and sociological features to cases of the Christian religion. Therefore, it is ultimately the similarity of the material appearance of the political movement (viz., its leader's character traits and its sociological features) to Christianity that lies at the center of scholars' definition of Maoism as being religious.

However, in my view, such an approach of studying religious Maoism is questionable because of two reasons. Firstly, since the degree of "similarity to Christianity" remains flexible, the definition of "being religious" in question would greatly expand the scope of "religious phenomena" in society so as to include potentially any collective social event led by charismatic leaders, which may even refer to events that are overtly anti-religious. In other words, such a definition of "being religious" may remain remote from our everyday use of the phrase and thus be quite counterintuitive in certain cases. Secondly, which is more important, the portrayal of material appearances of Maoism as being religious does not address its ideological nature. Ideologically, as the previous analysis of Maoist voluntarism indicates, Maoism forcefully opposes Christianity or any Christianity-like religion, and it takes nothing except the envisioned final stage of human history as the ultimate goal of individual and social transformation. Because of its all too immanent nature, it is problematic to characterize the ideology of Maoism as being religious.

To avoid these problematics in the study of religious Maoism, I shall stick to a stricter definition of "being religious" and seek somewhere else the religious foundation of the anti-rationalist nature of Maoist anti-intellectualism. In other words, for a comprehensive doctrine to be characterizable as "being religious," the doctrine needs to convey a transcendent ideal of ultimate transformation such that no identifiable state of individuals, societies, or human history can be perceived as a complete realization of such an ideal. With this stricter definition of being religious, I submit that one religious foundation of Maoist anti-intellectualism lies in a specific type of Ruism, viz., the school of heartmind led by Wang Yangming and his followers in late Ming Dynasty (1368–1644) of China.

I have three major arguments to support my claim that such a kind of Ruism comprises the religious foundation of Maoist anti-intellectualism:

Argument 1: the way Wang Yangming and his followers interpret Ru classics, mainly the *Great Learning* (大學, daxue), betokens a Ruist version of anti-intellectualism. This Ruist anti-intellectualism, which I'll call a Xinxue Anti-intellectualism (XA), is religious, homologically identical to major characteristics of Maoist voluntarism and historically precedes the latter.

Argument 2: the holistic and idealistic mindset of XA helped to shape the radically anti-Ruist attitude of westernized Chinese intellectuals in the period of New Cultural Movement and May Fourth Movement (1910s–1920s), who envisioned the masses' adoption of new and correct ideas from the West as the ultimate path to China's modernization. As growing from and sharing similar visions with such a cultural milieu, the young Mao Zedong's thought during this period was evidenced as having been greatly influenced by XA.

Argument 3: XA continued to influence Mao Zedong after 1920s. The Maoist utopian voluntarism rampant during the Cultural Revolution can be seen as resulting from a continuous application of the logic of XA to the issue of class struggle in the socialist movement of China, and hence, XA contributed to the religious cause of Maoist anti-intellectualism.

In the following, I will elaborate each of these arguments so as to compare them to the Trumpist anti-intellectualism.

Argument 1

Similar to the religious dimension of the Trumpist anti-intellectualism which ultimately rests upon a specific way of reading the Christian scripture, XA derives from a distinctive way of reading Ru classics. As I will indicate as follows, although Wang Yangming does not see ancient Ru classics as inerrant, his reading of them prioritizes how individuals apply their innate moral intuition to moments of everyday life over empirical knowledge of the outside world, which bears a strong resemblance to the second and third points of the evangelical biblical hermeneutics I generalized earlier.

The Ru classic the interpretation of which is at stake for my analysis of XA is quoted as follows:

> If an ancient person wished that all people under Heaven manifest their luminous virtues, he would first govern his state well. If he wished to govern his state well, he would first regulate his family. If he wished to regulate his family, he would first cultivate himself. If he wished to cultivate himself, he would first rectify his heartmind. If he wished to rectify his heartmind, he would first make his intentions sincere. If he wished to make his intentions sincere, he would first zhi zhi (致知, extend his knowledge or attain his conscientious awareness). zhi zhi consists in ge wu (格物, the investigation of things, or the rectification of things).[26]

The text was received by the Ru tradition as Confucius's own words which break down the Ru self-cultivation into eight steps: the grand goal of peace throughout the world rests upon the well-ordering of states, families, and the self-cultivation of each individual, which is furthermore elaborated as a process of the inner-work of human heartmind. The ultimate step is concerned with how to address the relationship of *zhi zhi* and *ge wu*, which I translate alternatively because the two different translations represent the greatest controversy of Ru thought in the time period of which we are concerned. For Zhu Xi and his followers in the school of pattern-principle (理學, lixue), *ge wu* means investigating empirically the ways how things in varying contexts dynamically and harmoniously fit together, which they call the "pattern-principles" of things. It is only after such empirical investigations that individuals are able to *zhi zhi*, viz., extend their moral knowledge about how to align their heartmind with outside realities so as to create layers of individual or social harmony aimed by the text. However, for Wang Yangming, such an empirical and piecemeal approach of self-cultivation is doomed to make scholars hypocritically not committed to practicing their words, as well as being susceptible of all other critiques in the quoted epigraph. Instead, Wang insists that *zhi zhi* should not come after *ge wu*. *Zhi zhi* means attaining one's innate moral consciousness, which Wang termed as "conscientious awareness" (良知, liangzhi) amenable to all major virtues taught traditionally by Ruism (such as humaneness, righteousness, and filial piety). *Ge wu* then means applying this innate conscientious awareness consistently to one's interactions with things and events in the world so as to "rectify" them to establish the desirable moral order in compliance with one's conscience. The following words best represent how Wang's construal of *zhi zhi* and *ge wu* can lead to serious suspicion towards empirical knowledge and hence to anti-intellectualism:

> Conscientious awareness does not exist because of what one sees and hears, while conscientious awareness can apply to all of what one sees and hears. Therefore, conscientious awareness is not restricted by one's seeing and hearing, but it is not apart from them either. . . . Outside of conscientious awareness, there is no other knowledge.[27]

Clearly, according to Wang, empirical knowledge of things outside the heartmind has no role whatsoever in *anchoring* one's self-cultivation. Wang Yangming's followers in late Ming Dynasty, the so-called left-wing school of heartmind, developed Wang's thought radically to an even utopian degree. For them, the innate knowledge of the good via one's conscientious awareness is "complete" (具足) and "continuously present" (見在) in each individual's heartmind.[28] Therefore, in reliance upon a method of mass education called "to enlighten the commoners for practicing the Way" (覺民行道),[29] these devoted followers of Wang Yangming went into suburbs, villages, and remote places of the country to inculcate Wang's teaching of conscientious awareness and stimulate individuals' will of moral self-cultivation in order to achieve the grand religious ambition that "Everyone filling the street is a sage."[30]

Careful readers may have already discovered why I stated XA as homologically equivalent to Maoist voluntarism: they both resort to mass education, and ultimately to the will of each individual in order to realize the allegedly correct ideas of individual and social transformation, although the content of these educations and ideas remain different. The religious nature of XA is conspicuous as well. Comparable to the Christian commitment to the transcendent goal of personal growth as being like Christ, Wang Yangming, following major teachings of traditional Ruism, considers the conscientious awareness as a manifestation of the cosmic Dao which ceaselessly generates novel things in the universe. Hence, via attaining conscientious awareness, Wang expects that one would constantly strive to become a sage who is a human exemplar of the cosmic Dao.[31]

Argument 2

Given the dominant influence of the Ruist statecraft stated by the *Great Learning* among traditionally educated intellectuals in late imperial China, it is no wonder why many of them turned into a radically anti-Ruist mindset during 1910s–1920s.

This is because the statecraft ties the success of a state firmly with whether individuals in the state are sincerely knowing a correct doctrine which provides comprehensive orientations to individual and social life. Hence, in face of the massive failure of the Chinese state triggered by the invasion of the colonial West, such a statecraft would drive dismayed intellectuals to totally abandon their tradition and hence seek alternative comprehensive doctrines from the invading Western powers.

In reality, such a holistic and idealistic statecraft did not affect China's social transformation once. As I argued somewhere else, it worked twice.[32] Pressured by domestic rebellions and national crises provoked by the invasion of regimes of ethnic minority, Ru literati launched a series of political and social reforms in Tang, Song through Ming Dynasties. The reforms underwent three stages to, respectively, focus upon literal techniques, political institutions, and the intellectual and moral state of each individual. This led to the rising of the Learning of Dao (道学, daoxue, commonly termed as "Neo-Confucianism" in English) as the dominant state ideology in late imperial China and concluded with a radical trend of moral utopianism in the left-wing school of heartmind analyzed earlier. Similarly, China's modernization after 1840s also experienced three stages: technological, institutional, and cultural, with the adoption of Marxism in the mainland of China as a conclusion. Understood as such, the final stage of China's modernization before China reopened to the West in late 1970s, viz., the Maoist utopian voluntarism during the Cultural Revolution, is nothing but a historical repetition of the holistic and idealistic Ru statecraft prescribed by the *Great Learning* and interpreted by XA.

However, in order to prove XA as indeed a religious cause of the Maoist anti-intellectualism, we need concrete evidences of the influence of Wang Yangming upon Mao's thought before he turned into Marxism. In this regard, two following quotes speak to such an influence decisively.

In the notes he took in college in 1913, Mao Zedong praised Confucius and Wang Yangming as equally "a man of transmitting (ancient) teaching" (傳教之人).[33] In addition, in a letter written in 1917 to a college teacher who also favored Wang's learning of heartmind, Mao says:

> If one wants to move the people under Heaven, one should move the heartmind of these people, and hence, cannot merely focus upon material manifestations (of the heartmind). If one wants to move the heartmind of the people, one must reply upon the fundamental root and origin. . . . The fundamental root and origin is the cosmic truth. The cosmic truth is located in the heartmind of each individual. . . . Nowadays, if we call on the people using the fundamental root and origin, can any heartmind under Heaven not be moved? If the heartmind under Heaven is all moved, can anything under Heaven not be done? If all things are done under Heaven, can our nation not be rich, powerful and happy?[34]

Despite the fact that in varying stages of Mao's thought the reference of "the cosmic truth" remains different, Mao's overall strategy of empowering the state via mobilizing the will of each individual to sincerely embrace a single correct comprehensive doctrine was formed, as indicated by the letter, in the earliest stage of Mao's thought. Because the semantics of the letter is extremely similar to the one of the *Great Learning* and Wang's interpretation of it, I have confidence to affirm Wang's significant influence upon Mao's young mind.

Therefore, regarding the ways how religions have shaped their anti-intellectualisms, Trump and Mao indicate similar and different characters. Mao is different from Trump in that Mao purposefully studied ancient Ru classics and Wang Yangming's thought in his youth, whereas Trump was not raised as an evangelical Christian and instead expected as a "baby Christian" by an influential evangelical Christian theologian during his presidential campaign.[35] However, the anti-intellectualisms of both Mao's and Trump's are clearly a product of the cultural and political movements in which they were so intensely involved. After all, I conclude that it would be as significant for us to understand the connection between XA, the New Cultural Movement, and the socialist movement led by Mao as it is to understand the interdependence between evangelical politics and the Trump presidency.

Argument 3

To indicate how XA continually influenced Mao's thought after Mao's youth, we shall just need to show how the XA logic of solving manifested social and national crises via a gradually deepening process of internalization, idealization, and radicalization continued to function on multiple facets of Maoism until the end of Mao's life. Two such examples are raised as follows.

Firstly, the attitude of Mao towards Confucius underwent radicalizing stages. As previously indicated, the young Mao knew Ru Classics "exceedingly well."[36] However, towards his middle age after the New Cultural Movement, Mao was increasingly critical of Confucius and saw "the veneration of Confucius" as an emblem of the "semi-feudal culture" of ancient China and thus of "the opposition of new culture and new thought."[37] Even so, Mao didn't entirely abandon Confucius's teaching and instead advocated to dialectically "inherit such a precious cultural heritage."[38] One example of this is that Mao urged his communist comrades to practice Ru virtues such as wisdom, benevolence, courage, loyalty, and righteous, yet to serve a communist cause.[39] Nevertheless, compounded by the fear of the threat from rising powers in the party such as Lin Biao, Mao launched the most ferocious anti-Confucian campaign at the last stage of Cultural Revolution. In other words, towards the end of his life, Mao's thought reached a final phase which pitted Ruism radically against his own voluntarist Marxist Maoism, viz., his final version of "the cosmic truth."

Secondly, a similar radicalizing process of Mao's thought can be found on his view of class struggle. In the early years of PRC, class struggle was treated by Mao mainly as an economic issue which got solved through political movements such as the land reform and the transformation of capitalist industries and commerce. However, as early as the anti-rightist movement in 1957, class struggle got addressed mainly politically so as to purge varying alleged enemies of the class of proletariat and peasants.[40] During the Cultural Revolution, the class struggle, seen increasingly as acute and violent, had become ideological, and "Mao became increasingly preoccupied with the pervasiveness of old values, ideas, and attitudes among the highest ranking Communist Party members."[41] Again, being subsequently economic, political, and ideological in nature, Mao's thought of class struggle follows the same logic of XA.

From these two examples, we can also compare how Trump and Mao utilized the anti-intellectual sources within their respective religious traditions to serve political purposes. The key method of Trump's citation of the Bible in political speeches is to quote it contextlessly, while applying biblical tropes directly to his political concerns of the moment, a method remarkably consistent with Pastor Lonnie's evangelical hermeneutics. Mao's application of XA to real politics was to strip it of any transcendent ideal which is supposed to be beyond the reach of any material reality, while keeping XA's holistic and idealist mindset so as to demand a perfect idealistic solution to pressuring problems at hand. Despite this apparent difference, both the Trumpist and Maoist anti-intellectualisms have committed the same religious fallacy, viz., they evoke religious ideals[42] unreflectively to justify and mobilize initiatives of mundane politics and hence unduly close the gap between religion and politics.

Conclusion: Antidotes

A certain suspicion towards the self-interest of intellectual elite while they pursue empirical knowledge is desirable, since firstly, this reflection is required by the spirit of rational criticism normally championed by such elite, and secondly, interests of varying social groups need to be harmonized for the sake of good governance. However, a religious foundation of the suspicion towards empirical knowledge acquired via the procedure of critical rationalism is by no means desirable. Empirical knowledge of objective reality is crucial to the survival and prosperity of any society whether the political regime of the society is a liberal democracy, an authoritarian socialist party-state, or an ancient imperial empire, three regimes addressed by this chapter. I see the Capitol riot in the United States on the January 6, 2021, and the rampant social chaos and economic collapse during the Cultural Revolution as the implosion of anti-intellectualist leadership of the Trumpist presidency and its precedent in the reign of Mao Zedong, although the scale of harm brought by the former is currently much less than the latter. As stressed earlier, albeit one among many factors to effect an overall anti-intellectual leadership, religious anti-intellectualism is capable of generating significant impact under certain favorable circumstances. Therefore, as a conclusion of this chapter, I feel obligated to say a few words about the antidote to each identified religious anti-intellectualism.

The way evangelicals read the Bible makes themselves susceptible to political manipulation (of which the Trump presidency furnishes ample evidences), because their biblical hermeneutics offers contextless exegesis, emphasizes personal application, and hence, ties their ultimate concern of salvation by the Christ directly and seamlessly with varying preliminary concerns addressed by public policies advocated by political groups. However, as my earlier definition of "being religious" implies, the value of religion as "ultimate concern"[43] consists in exactly that while providing comprehensive orientations to one's social and political engagement, religion transcends any concrete form of the engagement. This entails a double consciousness of religious people when they pursue politics: on the one hand, their religion shapes a moral consciousness to orient their advocacy of particular public policies; on the other hand, the religion should also keep them being critical of, and if necessary, attempting to revise any particular public policy since none of these policies is or will be adequate to the transcendent demand of faith in the ultimate sense. The careful gauging of whether or to what extent one supports a particular public policy clearly needs the ability of critical thinking and the respect towards empirical knowledge. So, I will cite a biblical verse to indicate why, for the sake of political engagement more beneficial for individuals and the society, evangelicals should not downplay the value of intellect: the belief in God doing His work dwells in "the evidence of the works themselves," and for Jesus's followers who are commanded by Jesus to "do even greater things"[44] than what Jesus did, they clearly need to think over more evidences about things in the world.

The case to make about the antidote to XA on the side of Ruism is less complicated since Wang's theoretical rival, the school of pattern-principle led by Zhu Xi's thought, offered an alternative interpretation of the classical Ru verses at stake. In order to prevent the reading of the *Great Learning* from devolving into that sort of ideological utopianism prevalent in the left-wing school of heartmind and in Maoist voluntarism, Zhu Xi's understanding of the relationship between the human heartmind and the pattern-principles of things in the world is a necessity. In other words, I advocate Zhu Xi's reading of the controversial verses in the *Great Learning* because, firstly, I do believe there are ecstatic moments during a Ru's religious practice of faith when his or her heartmind feels united with everything in the universe without being able to express such feeling in any discursive thought. Secondly, however, such a union of the heartmind with things in the universe can only happen momentarily under a certain circumstance. It does not imply that all pattern-principles of the universe have been absorbed by the heartmind, as Wang Yangming conceives it. Instead, the feeling of harmonious union, albeit being momentary and incomplete, shall motivate a Ru to continually investigate things in the world so as to increase the capacity of his or her heartmind to harmonize involved beings in evolving situations. In a word, the reading of the *Great Learning* along the lineage of Zhu Xi's thought can balance the commitment to the faith in the Cosmic Pattern-principle (天理, tianli) as a Ru's ultimate concern and the processual and concrete engagement with objective realities as his or her preliminary concerns. In an increasingly globalized and diversified world where the national crisis of China due to Western colonialism is no longer an emergency, the more empirical Ruism of Zhu Xi should be practiced more.

Notes

1 Mark Ward Sr., "'Knowledge Puffs Up': The Evangelical Culture of Anti-Intellectualism as a Local Strategy," *Sermon Studies*, vol. 4, no. 1 (2020), 12. The name of the studied pastor is changed.

2 Wang Yangming, *Instructions for Practical Living and Other Neo-Confucian Writings by Wang Yang-Ming*, trans. Wing-tsit Chan (New York and Landon: Columbia University Press, 1963), 122–123. The translation is adapted.

3 Ward, "'Knowledge Puffs Up'," 9.

4 "Confucianism" is a misnomer devised by early Christian missionaries in around the 19th century to refer to the Ru (儒, civilized human) tradition with a primary purpose of religious comparison and conversion, just as Islam was once called "Muhammadanism" in a similar historical context. Following the reflective scholarly trend upon the nomenclature, and in line with my other publications, "Confucianism" will be written as "Ruism" or "the Ru tradition," and "Confucian" or "Confucianist" will be written as "Ru" or "Ruist" in this chapter.

5 Ward, "'Knowledge Puffs Up'," 1–2.

6 One most informative research on the receptive history of Wang Yangming's moral philosophy in China and Japan can be found at 陈立胜 Chen Lisheng, "阳明学登场的几个历史时刻—当'王阳明'遭遇'现代性'" (Several Historical Moments of the Presence of the Learning of Yangming: When Wang Yangming Encounters Modernity), 《社会科学战线》, 2018 (07): 44–57. I follow the original language when quoting Chinese works titled either in traditional or simplified Chinese.

7 There is no sharp distinction between intellect and emotion in the traditional Ru understanding of the mind, and thus, 心 (xin), the center of human consciousness, is translated normally as "heartmind" in English scholarship.

8 A summary of such definitions can be found at Daniel Rigney, "Three Kinds of Anti-Intellectualism: Rethinking Hofstadter," *Sociological Inquiry*, vol. 61, no. 4 (November 1991), 435; Gretchen Ruecker Hoog, "The Liberal University and Its Perpetuation of Evangelical Anti-Intellectualism," *Seattle University Law Review*, vol. 33, no. 3 (2010), 690.

9 These three dimensions of American anti-intellectualism are categorized by Rigney, "Three Kinds," 434–451.

10 The connection between the anti-intellectual electorate and policies of the Trump presidency is studied by Matthew Motta, "The Dynamics and Political Implications of Anti-Intellectualism in the United States," *American Politics Research*, vol. 46, no. 3 (2018), 465–498.

11 Hoog, "The Liberal University," 695, quoting National Association of Evangelicals, *For the Health of the Nation: An Evangelical Call to Civil Responsibility* 1 (2004).

12 The fear of intellectualism is analyzed by Hoog, "The Liberal University," 691. The politics of fear among evangelicals is thematized by John Fea, *Believe Me, The Evangelical Road to Donald Trump* (Eerdmans, 2018).

13 Ward, "'Knowledge Puffs Up'," 5. All italics are original.

14 Michael Gerson, "The Last Temptation," *The Atlantic*, April 2018, www.theatlantic.com/magazine/archive/2018/04/the-last-temptation/554066/.

15 Carly Cassella, "Trump Cabinet Bible Study Teaches About the 'False Religion of Radical Environmentalism'," *Science Alert*, 5 April 2018, www.sciencealert.com/trump-cabinet-bible-study-teaches-about-the-false-religion-of-radical-environmentalism.

16 Laura Ellyn Smith, "The Spread of COVID-19 in the South Shows the Risks of Anti-intellectualism," *Washington Post*, 4 August 2020, www.washingtonpost.com/outlook/2020/08/04/spread-covid-19-south-shows-risks-anti-intellectualism/.

17 Ed Kilgore, "The Time Trump Got a Biblical Citation Very Wrong," *Intelligencer*, 17 December 2020, https://nymag.com/intelligencer/2020/12/the-time-trump-got-a-biblical-citation-very-wrong.html.

18 Christina Zhao, "Reverend Schools Trump by Quoting Bible, Tells President to 'Break with Your Sins and Start Living For Others'," *Newsweek*, 22 August 2019, www.newsweek.com/reverend-schools-trump-quoting-bible-tells-president-break-your-sins-start-living-others-1455817.

19 Ian Frazier, "Donald Trump and Uses and Misuses of the Bible," *The New Yorker*, 15 June 2020, www.newyorker.com/news/daily-comment/donald-trump-and-uses-and-misuses-of-the-bible.

20 Melissa Macauley, "To Understand Trump's GOP, We Need to Look to Lenin and Mao," *The Washington Post*, 1 November 2020, www.washingtonpost.com/outlook/2020/11/01/understand-trumps-gop-we-need-look-lenin-mao/. Another source on the similarity is Abigail Myers, "Those Who Fight and Those Who Write: Overthrowing the Elite and Their Institutions: Exploring Communist China & the United States" (Thesis, The University of Texas at Austin, 2017), 44–56.

21 Alana Wise, "'I Don't Think Science Knows': Visiting Fires, Trump Denies Climate Change," *NPR*, 14 September 2020, www.npr.org/2020/09/14/912799501/i-don-t-think-science-knows-visiting-fires-trump-denies-climate-change.

22 毛泽东 Mao Zedong, "对《在京艺术院校试行半工（农）半读》一文的批语 (A Comment on the Article 'An Experimentation of Half Worker (Peasant) Half Student in the Art Schools at Beijing')", 《建国以来毛泽东文稿》(北京：中央文献出版社，1998), 34–35. Translation is my own.

23 About Maoist Voluntarism, see Arif Dirlik, *Marxism in the Chinese Revolution* (New York: Rowman & Littlefield Publishers, 2005), 120–133; Maurice Meisner, *Marxism, Maoism and Utopianism* (Madison: The University of Wisconsin Press, 1982), 38–61, 89–109.

24 Joseph M. Kitagawa, "One of the Many Faces of China: Maoism as a Quasi-Religion," *Japanese Journal of Religious Studies*, vol. 1, no. 2/3 (June–September 1974), 125–141.

25 David E. Apter, "Bearing Witness: Maoism as Religion," *The Copenhagen Journal of Asian Studies*, vol. 22 (2005), 5–37. Rana Mitter, "Maoism in the Cultural Revolution: A Political Religion?" in *The Sacred in Twentieth-Century Politics*, ed. R. Griffin et al. (London: Palgrave Macmillan, 2008), 143–165.

26 This translation is adapted from Wing-Tsit Chan, trans. and ed., *A Source Book of Chinese Philosophy* (Princeton, NJ: Princeton University Press, 1936), 86. The use of

"he" highlights the importance of individual and keeps in line with the historical context, rather than showing any gender bias of the translator. My following analysis of Zhu Xi's and Wang Yangming's disparate interpretations is based upon my more extensive study on the text in Bin Song, "The Utopian Seed of Modern Chinese Politics in Ruism (Confucianism) and its Tillichian Remedy," in Thomas Bandy (ed.), *Why Tillich? Why Now?* (Atlanta, GA: Mercer University Press, 2021), 95–110.

27 Wang, *Instructions for Practical Living*, 150. The translation is adapted.

28 See 嵇文甫 Ji Wenfu, 左派王學 *The Left-wing School of Wang Yang-ming* (台北：萬卷樓出版社, 1990), 25–41; 钱明 Qian Ming, 阳明学的形成与发展 *The Formation and Development of the School of Wang Yang-ming* (南京：江苏古籍出版社, 2002), 172–176.

29 See 余英时 Yu Ying-shih, 宋明理學與政治文化 *Neo-Confucianism in Song and Ming and the Political Culture*, in 余英時文集 *Collected Works of Yu Ying-shih*, vol. 10(桂林：廣西師範大學出版社, 2006), 38.

30 Wang, *Instructions for Practical Living*, 240. Translation is adapted.

31 Wang's thought on this point is best represented by his four-sentence teaching. Please see Wang, *Instructions for Practical Living*, 243–245.

32 Song, "The Utopian Seed," 95–110.

33 毛泽东 Mao Zedong, "讲堂录" (Notes in Classrooms),毛泽东早期文稿 *Early Writings of Mao Zedong* (长沙：湖南出版社, 1990), 591. Translation is my own. 教 (teaching) is also used to translate "religion" in modern Chinese.

34 毛泽东 Mao Zedong, "致黎锦熙信" (A Letter to Li Jinxi), 毛泽东早期文稿 *Early Writings of Mao Zedong* (长沙：湖南出版社, 1990), 85–86.

35 James Dobson, "Dr. James Dobson on Donald Trump's Christian Faith," *Dr. James Dobson Family Institute*, www.drjamesdobson.org/news/dr-james-dobson-on-trumps-christian-faith, retrieved 29 May 2021.

36 Roland Boer, "Confucius and Chairman Mao: Towards a Study of Religion and Chinese Marxism," *Crisis and Critique*, vol. 2, no. 1 (2015), 40.

37 Boer, "Confucius," 39, quoting "On New Democracy" (1940) of Mao Zedong. Translation is adapted.

38 Boer, "Confucius," 44, quoting "On the New Stage" (1938) of Mao Zedong. Translation is adapted.

39 Boer, "Confucius," 48–49.

40 See A. James Gregor and Maria Hsia Chang, "Anti-Confucianism: Mao's Last Campaign," *Asian Survey*, vol. 19, no. 11 (November 1979), 1089.

41 Ibid.

42 According to the previous analysis, in Trump's case, the unreflectively evoked religious ideal is "being like Christ," as well as other related Christian goals. In Mao's case, it is the deeply Ruist one of "being willing to sincerely practice the cosmic truth," as well as other adapted Marxist ideals.

43 See Paul Tillich, *Systematic Theology*, vol. 1 (Chicago: University of Chicago Press, 1951), 11–14.

44 John 14:11–12, translation by the New International Version (NIV), www.biblica.com/bible/niv/john/14/.

9

FROM DOG WHISTLES TO FOG HORNS

Richard Nixon, Donald Trump, and Their Silent Majorities

Sarah Thelen

Shortly after Donald J. Trump descended his golden escalator on 16 June 2015, to announce that he would run for President in 2016, signs proclaiming that "The Silent Majority Stands With Trump" appeared in yards across the country. Despite polling showing a clear advantage for his opponent, Trump and his supporters argued for the existence of a group of "silent" Trump voters overlooked by the national media and/or unwilling to publicly state their support for Trump. And, in the end, it was Trump, not the Democratic candidate, and favourite, Hillary Clinton, who would move into the White House in January 2017. That neither candidate received a majority of the votes and that Trump's supporters were, as a rule, the opposite of silent did not diminish the appeal and power of the *idea* of a Silent Majority in both Trump's rhetoric and in how his supporters saw themselves. The resonance of this political identity echoed an earlier politician who used the idea of a Silent Majority to divide the population to his own political advantage: President Richard Nixon. In both 1969 and 2016, this appeal was a powerful one amongst amidst dramatic social and economic changes. And while white, working-class supporters of both presidents became the focus of media efforts to understand the phenomenon, the Silent Majority's appeal reached—and reaches—far beyond this group. Just as Nixon had the support of wealthy elites and intellectuals as well as the so-called "Hard Hats," so too did Trump's Silent Majority include upper middle class and wealthy suburbanites.

Which, then and now, is an unlikely combination, but Trump's canny use of divisive patriotic appeals followed the path set down by Nixon and both presidents' use of a weaponised patriotism to divide the nation and mobilise their supporters is, perhaps, their most dangerous parallel. The United States has long had a complicated and often contentious relationship with patriotism and national identity with tensions escalating when a group that sees itself as

DOI: 10.4324/9781003110361-9

the "true" Americans feels threatened by the progress and advancement of other groups.[1] The racial and economic elements of the patriotism promoted by both Nixon and Trump reflect this dynamic as both men transformed their supporters' fears into votes. And with the animus both inspire, it can be tempting to see Trump as a political reincarnation of the 37th President, but the situation is far more complicated. For while they have definite similarities—thin-skins, vindictiveness, and unhesitating pursuit of control—they are, at the end of the day, very different people. Trump ran as the ultimate outsider, a reality TV star and real estate tycoon with no political experience, while Nixon's successful 1968 presidential run emphasised his political and diplomatic experience and, indeed, painted him as an elder statesman—someone best positioned to manage the complicated international and domestic situation he would inherit.[2] In this way, Nixon offered voters change but within conventional political bounds—much the way that any member of an out-of-power political party would. Nixon argued that the Democrats had had their chance and had only made the situation worse in Vietnam and at home, but it was a far cry from Trump's charges of "American carnage" at his 2017 Inauguration.

Thus, rather than a return to Nixon, Trump represents the ways Nixon's own political rhetoric reshaped the nation. Even as Nixon modulated the extremism of a Wallace or a Goldwater, he normalised the underlying sentiments. His coded appeals to "law and order" and invocation of traditional values helped his target audience see themselves as the sole protectors of American values and, in doing so, laid the foundations for Trump's eventual victory. Trump, in turn, pushed the limits of these norms—indeed, breaking many in the process—and as more than one commentator noted, "said the quiet part out loud,"[3] which was as gratifying to his supporters as it was shocking to his opponents. In this way, Trump's presidency reminds us how much of US democracy depends on mutually agreed norms rather than law to function and of how vulnerable those norms can be. Trump and his supporters trampled over so many of those norms that it is very tempting to cast them as a sharp break or aberration when, in actuality, they are the logical consequences of a system which had long contorted itself so as to accommodate voters from across the political spectrum ranging from civil rights activists to segregationists, liberals to conservatives, flag burners to the American Legion. While neither the first nor the last attempt to unite one side of this equation, Nixon's Silent Majority was an important moment when the president explicitly appealed to a very particular patriotism to rally supporters and isolate opponents. And its parallels with Trump's presidency make it a particularly enlightening one.

★ ★ ★

Having himself benefitted from domestic opposition to the Vietnam War when campaigning against Vice President Hubert Humphrey in 1968, Nixon arrived in the White House determined to ensure that future challengers would not have a similar advantage. Shortly after his victory, his foreign policy team—including recent recruit Dr. Henry Kissinger—explored military and diplomatic options for the war. Following their advice, Nixon would adopt a policy of "Vietnamization" intended to limit US casualties and bring US troops home while still ensuring the survival of South Vietnam.[4] At the same time, he would continue efforts to reach a negotiated settlement but knew that such an agreement would require quieting domestic dissent. As Nixon described it, the anti-war movement and mounting domestic protests and opposition encouraged the North Vietnamese to simply wait out the United States, confident that domestic opposition would eventually force a US withdrawal.[5] Furthermore, Nixon was determined to isolate and undermine the anti-war movement so as to avoid the fate of President Lyndon Johnson who, by the end of his term, faced near-constant protests and heckling whenever he left the White House. As part of this effort, Nixon gave what would become a landmark speech in November 1969.

Sitting at his desk in the Oval Office the night of 3 November 1969, President Nixon looked into the television cameras and argued that the United States was making progress in Vietnam. He described the situation when he took office and then outlined the steps he had taken to withdraw US troops and negotiate an end to the conflict. Essentially a conventional speech, few would remember it if not for the unusual closing. Instead of ending his speech with a request for national support, Nixon spoke directly to "the great silent majority of my fellow Americans," who, presumably shared his views on the Vietnam War.[6] Those words inspired an avalanche of supportive letters and telegrams from self-proclaimed members of the silent majority from across the United States. Revelling in this tangible demonstration of popular support years later, Nixon recalled: "it was one thing to make a rhetorical appeal to the Silent Majority—it was another to actually hear from them."[7]

The outpouring of support after the speech was all the more gratifying as it came in the midst of a significant expansion of the anti-war movement. Just over two weeks before Nixon addressed the nation, on 15 October 1969, the anti-war movement staged the incredibly successful Moratorium protest. Not only did the Moratorium protests involve more people in more locations than any previous anti-war protest, but they also showcased the increasingly mainstream nature of the anti-war movement. When planning the October protests, activists intended to demonstrate that they were not "just 'crazy radicals'" but, rather, represented a large cross-section of the US population.[8] And, by this metric, the 15 October Moratorium protests were incredibly successful. Thousands of Americans of all ages and from all walks of life—not just the "usual" student radicals showcased in media coverage of the movement—took part in teach-ins, marches, and other events intended to demonstrate their opposition to the US war in Vietnam. To encourage this broad participation, planners organised countless local events so that people could participate without needing to travel to a major city or otherwise inconvenience themselves. The goal was, essentially, to make it as easy as possible for as many people as possible to participate and they succeeded, much to the administration's chagrin. Nixon and his supporters had worked very hard through much of 1969 to frame the anti-war movement as predominantly made up of extremist students and the sight of teachers, business people, housewives, and other seemingly "average" Americans threatened to undermine their efforts.

The administration had, of course, worked to counter the October protests, but while they had been "moderately successful" in creating visible support, a White House aide concluded that they had "no reason to be satisfied or smug."[9] He went on to argue that they could have "easily eclipsed" the Moratorium protests had they simply "started earlier and . . . been better coordinated" and recommended that the White House start planning immediately for the 15 November protests.[10] Nixon, Chief of Staff Haldeman, and other senior staffers agreed and the White House soon had a detailed plan for its counter-programming for the November protests. Furthermore, the report concluded that with proper time, attention, and resources, they could well overshadow upcoming protests. It, therefore, went on to recommend a much more proactive and carefully planned effort to counter the November protests. Nixon agreed and aides started planning their counter-programming for the November protests almost immediately.[11]

The centrepiece of these plans was the President's 3 November speech. Originally scheduled to strengthen a secret ultimatum to the North Vietnamese, the speech provided Nixon and his staff with an excellent opportunity to reframe the domestic debate over Vietnam.[12] And so, Nixon addressed the nation on 3 November seeking to convince them that he was making progress in Vietnam and, more importantly, would *continue* making progress as long as the country supported him. He emphasised the importance of domestic public opinion and implied that defeat was only possible through internal surrender: "for North Vietnam cannot defeat or humiliate the United States. Only Americans can do that."[13] Framing domestic dissent and opposition as implicitly un-American and unpatriotic, Nixon sought to marginalise the increasingly mainstream protest movement. It was his unique closing, though, that would prove most effective. By appealing to a so-called "silent majority," Nixon cast the war's opponents as a minority, encouraged his supporters to see themselves as part of a larger group, and framed dissent as a betrayal.

His words struck a nerve and self-proclaimed members of the Silent Majority soon became very loud indeed. While Nixon and his aides consistently framed this support as spontaneous, it is important to note that it was being planned even before Nixon's speech was announced.[14] Even predating the speech itself in some cases. Or, rather, the intention to inspire a response pre-dated the speech itself. That it took the form of an enthusiastic embrace of the Silent Majority surprised even the president. Meeting Nixon shortly after the speech, speechwriter William Safire asked about the phrase and the president "shrugged" and told him "if he had thought it would be picked up, he said, he would have capitalized it in the speech text."[15]

Rather, much of the White House planning before the speech intended to promote the idea of a "Crusade for Peace" but lent itself equally well to the Silent Majority idea once it was clear how popular the term had become.[16] In the weeks leading up to the speech, aides laid the foundation for a groundswell of seemingly spontaneous popular support. They made arrangements with Western Union for telegrams, prepared surrogates with statements encouraging people to write, wire, or phone the White House and other politicians to express their support.[17] Now clearly recognisable as an "astroturf," or fake grassroots, campaign, the White House efforts were incredibly successful. The idea of astroturfing public opinion did not become well known until Texas Senator Lloyd Bentsen coined the term in 1985 in response to insurance industry efforts to fight regulation. But, as the response to Nixon's Silent Majority speech shows, the practice was well established long before Benson's observation. In Nixon's case, his staff's preparations resulted in nearly 2,000 more telegrams in the week after the speech than in the week before and an eventual White House tally of 208,886 "known supporters."[18] More importantly, the visible Silent Majority support enabled Nixon and his supporters to reframe the domestic debate over the war.

★ ★ ★

With covert encouragement from the Nixon White House, the Silent Majority took to the streets in November 1969. Many joined a range of local National Unity Week events intended to demonstrate support for Nixon's Vietnam policies and, perhaps more importantly, a rejection of the anti-war movement's own events. Organised by the Committee for a Week of National Unity and the National Committee for Responsible Patriotism, the events were local and relatively understated since organisers felt that most Americans "believed that the president was doing all he could to end the war, but did not want to have to parade in the streets to show their support."[19] And so, instead of the teach-ins and protests of the anti-war Mobilisation, most members of the Silent Majority participated by displaying the flag on "offices, homes, automobile bumpers and windshields, lapel pins" and so forth as well as turning on their "porch lights and automobile headlights during daylight hours."[20] Organisers also planned a "series of patriotic rallies throughout the country," most scheduled to coincide with Veterans' Day on 11 November.[21] Watching these parades, a *Newsweek* journalist reported that "many turned out even without encouragement from official Washington" and noted that the Department of Veterans' Affairs had sent out 100,000 of "Veterans' Day kits" across the country. Even more importantly, a participant proudly declared that "there are more of us patriotic Americans than those pro-Hanoicrats."[22]

Always careful to maintain the image of grassroots enthusiasm, White House officials carefully monitored these events and sought to influence and control them to the best of their abilities. They were certainly pleased with the popularity of the Silent Majority idea and were eager to capitalise on it to the president's advantage—indeed, by the end of the month, Chief of Staff H.R. Haldeman sent an internal memo advising all White House staff that their work should, "As a general rule, . . . be tied to the 'Silent Majority' over and over . . . always."[23] White House officials hoped to use the Silent Majority to demonstrate to the North Vietnamese that Nixon did, indeed, have the domestic support necessary to back up his threats to stay in Vietnam until US demands were met. They also planned to use this evidence of Silent Majority support to undermine and marginalise the anti-war movement. By carefully avoiding specifics about Nixon's Vietnam policies, both he and the nascent Silent Majority framed their actions as demonstrations of a more general, and ostensibly nonpartisan, patriotic support for the president. In statements about the Vietnam War and even when campaigning for Republican candidates in 1970, Nixon consistently presented himself as an apolitical figure simply trying to do what was best for the country. And, by implication, those who opposed him were the true threats.

The Silent Majority's energy and enthusiasm waned over time, not least because, as Haldeman later noted, most of them "weren't activists" even though Nixon and his staff repeatedly tried to, in Haldeman's recollection, "help them along."[24] But, in some ways, Nixon's initial efforts at isolating and undermining the anti-war movement proved too successful for maintaining a mobilised Silent Majority. With troops coming home from Vietnam, casualties declining, and anti-war organisations packing up their offices,[25] many in the Silent Majority likely felt they had done their part by early spring 1970. But just when both the anti-war movement and the Silent Majority seemed to be fading away, Nixon announced US incursions into Cambodia reigniting the fury and energy of both sides. Anti-war activists in Washington, DC, took breaks from packing up the Moratorium offices to watch Nixon's 30 April 1970 speech and were soon scrambling to coordinate protests in response to the announcement.[26] And even as anti-war activists flocked to Washington, DC, protests broke out across the nation, with students at the forefront. These came to a head less than a week after Nixon's announcement as violence broke out on the campuses. On 4 May, members of the Ohio National Guard fired into a group of protesters, killing four and wounding nine others. The deaths at Kent State, an untimely comment from Nixon calling protesters "bums" three days earlier, and another deadly confrontation with two students killed and twelve wounded at Jackson State in Mississippi less than two weeks later complicated White House efforts to "avoid having the blame land on us."[27]

★ ★ ★

Even as the White House struggled to manage reactions to the apparent escalation in Vietnam, the Silent Majority surged into action. Only days after the Kent State tragedy, construction workers and other blue-collar union members flooded down New York City's Wall Street during their lunch break to confront participants in a vigil honouring the Kent State victims. Waving flags and brandishing pipes, wrenches, and other tools, they converged on the anti-war activists ultimately sending eleven protesters to the hospital and injuring countless hours during the three-hour melee.[28] While they officially deplored the violence of the so-called Hard Hats, Nixon and his aides privately celebrated their actions. Not only did the Hard Hat riots—and a peaceful march later in the month—strengthen Nixon's claims to speak for a Silent Majority of citizens who supported him, supported the Vietnam War, and opposed the anti-war movement, but this particular subset of the Silent Majority also had long been a Democratic bulwark.

As Jefferson Cowie notes in *Stayin' Alive*, the 1970s marked a dramatic shift in the socioeconomic—and therefore political—trajectory of the white working class.[29] Nixon's Silent Majority was an important first step in the movement of that group from Democratic bastions to the core of an increasingly populist Republican party. Starting with the explicitly racist appeals of Wallace and Goldwater, moderated and expanded by Nixon's coded appeals, the Republican Party gradually replaced the Democrats as the dominant party in the South. These Republican successes encouraged politicians to hew ever closer to the racialised and nationalist appeals central to Nixon's Silent Majority culminating in Trump's jingoistic, exclusive patriotism. This particular patriotism was on proud display in the May 1970 Hard Hat protests and these newly enthusiastic supporters were a political dream come true for the president. Not only were new allies always welcome, but this group was also an almost perfect match for the "unyoung, unpoor, and unblack; . . . middle-aged, middle-class, middle-minded"[30] voters Democratic political advisors Richard Scammon and Ben Wattenberg had urged their party colleagues to target in the 1970s. Never one to overlook canny political advice—even if intended for the other side—Nixon, therefore, urged his staff to both read the book and then to come up with plans for how he (and the Republican Party) could secure the loyalty of this group ahead of the Democrats.

The outpouring of Hard Hat support for Nixon after the resurgence of protest in response to the Cambodia announcements was a gratifying sign that they were succeeding. In their enthusiasm, aides often glossed over the violence of the initial Hard Hat riots, noting instead that

> What we saw in New York on Friday was the first manifestation of a willingness to fight for the America the blue collar American loves: an America where people work for a living, where they respect the flag, where they appreciate what they have.[31]

Although noting that the violence was "deplorable," the aide strongly encouraged active cultivation of this group. Another White House aide argued that "properly controlled and channeled (sic)," even such violent support could "be molded (sic) into a positive and constructive movement."[32]

While certainly more formal and, indeed, measured than much of the communications issuing from the Trump White House in January 2021, the shared sentiments are clear. Violence from supporters was acceptable and even to be encouraged in the effort to counter the opposition. And while Trump did not invite the leaders of the groups who stormed the Capitol on 6 January to the White House, it is likely only because he would not be residing there for much longer. And doubtless, had he invited them, he would not have waited until after a peaceful rally or been at pains to emphasise the nonviolent aspects of their support as Nixon was in June 1970.[33] Rather, Trump actively celebrated and encouraged the self-proclaimed "Stop the Steal" protesters. First, in a speech at the Ellipse near the White House that morning in which he not only told his audience that "if you don't fight like hell, you're not going to have a country anymore" but also promises that "I'll be there with you" as the group prepared to march to the Capitol.[34] And later in Tweets and public statements reiterating his claims of a stolen election and celebrating his patriotic supporters. The violent insurrection, actively encouraged by a sitting President, is perhaps the most striking legacy of Nixon's own efforts to politicise patriotism by cultivating a Silent Majority.

★ ★ ★

Trump, unlike Nixon, did not have to shepherd his Silent Majority into existence. Rather, many of its members in 2016 likely remembered Nixon's earlier appeals and, if not, the idea was doubtless familiar. And so, confident in their support, Trump pushed the envelope of what was acceptable in the US political discourse. In debates and rallies, in public statements, interviews, and on Twitter, he mocked his opponents' wives, crudely invoked his masculinity, threatened journalists with physical violence, ridiculed physical disabilities, made vulgar comments about women, and so forth until it seemed nothing was off-limits. Including promises to keep Mexican rapists, "drug lords," and other "bad hombres" out of the United States.[35]

Once in office, Trump continued to court his white supporters and repeatedly failed to challenge, much less distance himself from, white supremacists. It took significant political and social pressure to get Trump, who as a New York real estate mogul had taken out a full-page ad endorsing the racist trial of the Central Park Seven, to even mildly critique his supporters, leading to half-hearted comments deploring violence, but still arguing that there were "very fine people, on both sides" after a white supremacist drove into a group of counterprotesters during the August 2017 Unite the Right rally in Charlottesville, South Carolina killing Heather Heyer.[36] Two years later, Trump angrily tweeted that Representatives Alexandria Ocasio-Cortez (D-NY), Ilhan Omar (D-MN), Ayanna Pressley (D-MA), and Rashida Tlaib (D-MI) should "go back and help fix the totally broken and crime infested places from which they came" instead of criticising his policies, adding in a subsequent Tweet that the women "can't leave fast enough."[37] Trump's comments reflect a stand of the US national identity in which immigrants, naturalised citizens, and their children can never be fully American. Especially if, as in this case, the US citizens in question do not fit the mental image of a "typical"—meaning white—American. And so, Trump's comments to a Puerto Rican woman from New York, to a Somali immigrant and naturalised citizen, a Black woman, and a Palestinian woman from Detroit reflected a belief shared among many of Trump's supporters. And, indeed, with many in Nixon's Silent Majority as well, who responded to anti-war protesters and other critics with chants of "Love it or Leave it."[38]

Like their respective supporters, both Trump and Nixon share an exclusionary understanding of both patriotism and the US identity. And, they are far from alone. Survey responses and voting patterns repeatedly demonstrated that a significant majority of the US citizens—regardless of their party identification—share a narrow view of what makes someone "truly American."[39] Specifically, such a person must be Christian, speak English, and have been born in the United States. Unsurprisingly, such nationalists also hold negative views of immigration, as do both Nixon's and Trump's supporters. Claiming that this group is a "Silent Majority" suited both presidents as it enabled them to simultaneously appeal to a sense of grievance as well as reassure their devotees that they are still a dominant force. This combination of grievance and confidence goes far toward explaining how many in the mob storming the Capitol on 6 January 2021, described themselves as "patriots" even while participating in an armed insurrection and invading the US Capitol.

Notes

1 Merle Curti, *The Roots of American Loyalty* (New York: Columbia University Press, 1946); John Fousek, *To Lead the Free World: American Nationalism and the Cultural Roots of the Cold War* (Chapel Hill: University of North Carolina Press, 2000); Robert Justin Goldstein, *Saving Old Glory: The History of the American Flag Desecration Controversy* (Boulder, CO: Westview Press, 1995); Jonathan M. Hansen, *The Lost Promise of Patriotism: Debating American Identity, 1890–1920* (Chicago: University of Chicago Press, 2003); Michael G. Kammen, *Mystic Chords of Memory: The Transformation of Tradition in American Culture* (New York: Knopf, 1991); Cecilia Elizabeth O'Leary, *To Die For: The Paradox of American Patriotism* (Princeton, NJ: Princeton University Press, 1999); Woden Teachout, *Capture the Flag: A Political History of American Patriotism* (New York, NY: Basic Books, 2009); Arnaldo Testi, *Capture the Flag: The Stars and Stripes in American History* (New York: New York University Press, 2010); David Waldstreicher, *In the Midst of Perpetual Fetes: The Making of American Nationalism,*

1776–1820 (Chapel Hill: Published for the Omohundro Institute of Early American History and Culture, Williamsburg, Virginia, by the University of North Carolina Press, 1997).

2 David Greenberg, *Nixon's Shadow: The History of an Image* (New York: W.W. Norton, 2003); Joe McGinniss, *The Selling of the President* (Harmondsworth: Penguin, 1970); Melvin Small, "The Election of 1968," *Diplomatic History*, vol. 28, no. 4 (September 1, 2004), 513–528, https://doi.org/10.1111/j.1467-7709.2004.00428.x; Theodore H. White, *The Making of the President, 1968* (New York: Atheneum Publishers, 1969).

3 See, for example: Eli Stokols, "'Saying the Quiet Part Out Loud': Trump Says What Other Presidents Only Thought, or Never Would Think," *Los Angeles Times*, 7 September 2018, www.latimes.com/politics/la-na-pol-trump-impolitic-outbursts-20180907-story.html.

4 Jeffrey P. Kimball, *Nixon's Vietnam War* (Lawrence, KS: University Press of Kansas, 1998); David L. Prentice, "Choosing 'the Long Road': Henry Kissinger, Melvin Laird, Vietnamization, and the War Over Nixon's Vietnam Strategy," *Diplomatic History*, vol. 40, no. 3 (June 2016), 445–74, https://doi.org/10.1093/dh/dhv002.

5 Kimball, *Nixon's Vietnam War*; Henry Kissinger, *White House Years* (Boston: Little, Brown, 1979); Sarah Thelen, "The Importance of Being Popular: Richard Nixon, Henry Kissinger, and Domestic Support for the Vietnam War," in David Fitzgerald, David Ryan, and John M Thompson (eds.), *Not Even Past: How the United States Ends Wars* (New York: Berghan Books, 2020), 21–44.

6 Richard Nixon, "Address to the Nation on the War in Vietnam," 3 November 1969, Online by Gerhard Peters and John T. Woolley, *The American Presidency Project*, www.presidency.ucsb.edu/ws/?pid=2303.

7 "'Resume' of the November 3rd Speech Game Plan," n.d., 2, Silent Majority; Box 1; WHCF: SMOF Butterfield, NPLM, College Park, MD; Richard Nixon, *RN: The Memoirs of Richard Nixon* (London: Sidgwick and Jackson, 1978), 410.

8 Tom Wells, *The War Within: America's Battle Over Vietnam* (Berkeley, CA: University of California Press, 1994), 330.

9 "Charles West to Alex Butterfield," n.d., Memoranda Received Oct thru Dec 1969; Box 8; WHSF: SMOF Butterfield, NPLM, College Park, MD.

10 "Charles West to Alex Butterfield."

11 "Alex Butterfield to Jeb Magruder [1]," 17 October 1969, Memos/Alex Butterfield (October 1969); Box 53; WHSF: SMOF Haldeman, NPLM, College Park, MD; "Alex Butterfield to H.R. Haldeman," 24 October 1969, Memos/Alex Butterfield (November 1969); Box 54; WHSF: SMOF Haldeman, NPLM, College Park, MD; "William Safire to H.R. Haldeman," 22 October 1969, Memoranda Received Oct thru Dec 1969; Box 8; WHSF: SMOF Butterfield, NPLM, College Park, MD.

12 Thelen, "The Importance of Being Popular."

13 Nixon, "Address to the Nation on the War in Vietnam."

14 For a full discussion of White House efforts around the Silent Majority speech, see: Sarah Thelen, "Mobilizing a Majority: Nixon's 'Silent Majority' Speech and the Domestic Debate over Vietnam," *Journal of American Studies*, vol. 51, no. 3 (August 2017), 887–914, https://doi.org/10.1017/S0021875816001936.

15 William Safire, *Before the Fall: An Inside View of the Pre-Watergate White House* (Garden City, NY: Doubleday, 2005), 175.

16 "William Safire to H.R. Haldeman"; "Dick Garbett to Alex Butterfield," 27 October 1969, Memoranda Received Oct thru Dec 1969; Box 8; WHSF: SMOF Butterfield, NPLM, College Park, MD; "H.R. Haldeman to William Safire, Lyn Nofziger, Jeb

Magruder, Dwight Chapin, Ron Zeigler, Herb Klein, Harry Dent, Kenneth Cole, Alex Butterfield, Margita White, John R. Brown, Charles Colson, Connie Stuart, Jim Keogh," 6 November 1969, Memos/Jeb Magruder (November 1969); Box 54; WHSF: SMOF Haldeman, NPLM, College Park, MD.

17 "Game Plan for the President's November 3rd Speech on Vietnam, Master Copy," n.d., Silent Majority; Box 1; WHCF: SMOF Butterfield, NPLM, College Park, MD; "Game Plan for the President's November 3rd Speech on Vietnam—Game Plan in Four Phases," n.d., Memos/Alex Butterfield (November 1969); Box 54; WHSF: SMOF Haldeman, NPLM, College Park, MD; "Dwight Chapin to Alex Butterfield," 22 October 1969, Memoranda Received Oct thru Dec 1969; Box 8; WHSF: SMOF Butterfield, NPLM, College Park, MD.

18 Brandon Rottinghaus, "'Dear Mr. President': The Institutionalization and Politicization of Public Opinion Mail in the White House," *Political Science Quarterly*, vol. 121, no. 3 (2006), 451–76.

19 Sandra Scanlon, *The Pro-War Movement: Domestic Support for the Vietnam War and the Making of Modern American Conservatism* (Amherst, MA: University of Massachusetts Press, 2013), 190.

20 "Alex Butterfield to Richard Nixon," 12 November 1969, 1, Memoranda for The President's File (November 1969); Box 138; WHSF: SMOF Haldeman, NPLM, College Park, MD.

21 "Alex Butterfield to Richard Nixon," 1.

22 "Love It or . . . Leave It," *Newsweek*, 24 November 1969, Silent Majority; Box 1; WHCF: SMOF Butterfield, NPLM, College Park, MD.

23 "H.R. Haldeman to Jeb Magruder [2]," 21 November 1969, Memos/Jeb Magruder (November 1969); Box 54; WHSF: SMOF Haldeman, NPLM, College Park, MD.

24 Wells, *The War Within*, 386.

25 Aaron Latham, "Vietnam Moratorium Headquarters Closes," *The Washington Post, Times Herald (1959–1973); Washington, D.C.*, 2 May 1970.

26 Ibid.

27 "Charles Colson to H.R. Haldeman," 6 May 1970, HRH Memos 1969–70 (Complete) [1 of 3]; Box 1; WHSF: SMOF Colson, NPLM, College Park, MD. Nixon made his infamous "bums" comment during a 1 May, 1970, visit to the Pentagon. Juan de Onis, "Nixon Puts 'Bums' Label On Some College Radicals: NIXON DENOUNCES 'BUMS' ON CAMPUS," *New York Times*, 2 May 1970; "The President's News Conference," 8 May 1970, www.presidency.ucsb.edu/documents/the-presidents-news-conference-144.

28 Michael Drosnin, "After 'Bloody Friday,' New York Wonders If Wall Street Is Becoming a Battleground," *Wall Street Journal (1923—Current File); New York, N.Y.*, 11 May 1970; "Protesters' Ranks Grow: Fervor Spreads On Eve Of Washington Mass Rally," *The Sun (1837–1992); Baltimore, Md.*, 9 May 1970.

29 Jefferson Cowie, *Stayin' Alive: The 1970s and the Last Days of the Working Class* (New York, NY: New Press, 2010).

30 Richard M. Scammon and Ben J. Wattenberg, *The Real Majority* (New York: Coward-McCann, 1970), 21.

31 "Tom Huston to Bryce Harlow, Harry Dent, Lyn Nofziger, Murray Chotiner, H.R. Haldeman, and John Ehrlichman," 15 May 1970, 4, HRH Memoranda For The President May 1970; Box 139; WHSF: SMOF Haldeman, NPLM, College Park, MD.

32 "Steve Bull to Charles Colson," 22 May 1970, Hard Hats; Box 69; WHSF: SMOF Colson, NPLM, College Park, MD.

33 "Memorandum to Richard Nixon," n.d., Hard Hats; Box 20; WHSF: SMOF Colson, NPLM, College Park, MD; "Charles Colson for the President's File," September 12, 1970, Hard Hats; Box 20; WHSF: SMOF Colson, NPLM, College Park, MD.

34 "Read Trump's Jan. 6 Speech, A Key Part Of Impeachment Trial," *NPR.org*, accessed 21 May 2021, www.npr.org/2021/02/10/966396848/read-trumps-jan-6-speech-a-key-part-of-impeachment-trial.

35 "Transcript of the Third Debate—The New York Times," accessed 14 May 2021, www.nytimes.com/2016/10/20/us/politics/third-debate-transcript.html.

36 Donald J. Trump, "Bring Back the Death Penalty. Bring Back Our Police! (Full-Page Advertisement)," *The New York Times*, 1 May 1989, sec. New York; Donald J. Trump, "Remarks on Infrastructure and an Exchange With Reporters in New York," 15 August 2017, www.presidency.ucsb.edu/documents/remarks-infrastructure-and-exchange-with-reporters-new-york-city.

37 Trump has since been permanently suspended from Twitter but the full text of his tweets can be found both in media coverage and by keyword search at the Trump Twitter Archive. See, e.g., Katie Rogers and Nicholas Fandos, "Trump Tells Congresswomen to 'Go Back' to the Countries They Came From," *The New York Times*, 14 July 2019, sec. U.S., www.nytimes.com/2019/07/14/us/politics/trump-twitter-squad-congress.html.

38 "Love It or . . . Leave It"; Drosnin, "After 'Bloody Friday,' New York Wonders If Wall Street Is Becoming a Battleground"; "John Volpe to L.P. Gilvin," 23 June 1970, Hard Hats; Box 69; WHSF: SMOF Colson, NPLM, College Park, MD; Martin Weil, "Divergent Views Mingle Happily at Folklife Festival," *The Washington Post, Times Herald (1959–1973); Washington, D.C.*, 5 July 1970, sec. General.

39 Bart Bonikowski and Paul DiMaggio, "Varieties of American Popular Nationalism," *American Sociological Review*, vol. 81, no. 5 (October 2016), 972, https://doi.org/10.1177/0003122416663683.

10

CONCLUSION

In the Twilight of Trump's Idols

Mark A. Menaldo and Michael Harvey

This book has a simple thesis: *This has all happened before*. The unlikely rise and extraordinary presidency of Donald Trump are a new American experience but an old story in the life of democracies and other polities. What effect may this Plutarch-inspired perspective on Donald Trump have on readers? Well, to the extent that the chapters in this book constitute an argument about the danger of populist leadership for stable democracy, we hope to have persuaded some readers of the real prospect of that danger.[1] In today's polarized reality, our readership is likely limited to readers disposed to be sympathetic to a broadly anti-Trump perspective. But we hope to speak beyond that group, to Trump's defenders and beyond. In the first part of our conclusion, we address Trump defenders' presumptive criticisms of our volume. In the second part, we speak to the scholarly and lay readers who see value in these chapters, who are civically inclined to think about what Trump has wrought, and what remedies might be available to repair the damage to American society, and American political institutions, in particular.

To Donald Trump's defenders, our chapters will read as hyperbole, expressions of snobbish disdain for Donald Trump. Trump's defenders might say that what we decry so loudly about Trump in this volume is merely an oversensitive overreaction to his flouting of norms: the modern equivalent of Andrew Jackson opening the White House to the public. They might say that we don't have the stomach for his defining traits: boldness and combativeness.[2] We will even support their criticism by pointing to Thomas Hobbes's astute observation that people often confuse manners with morals.[3] Trump may have bad manners, his defenders argue, but he is, at core, and especially as a leader, not immoral. The problem is not with Trump but with us, the authors of this volume, who cannot get over our Plutarchian sensibilities.

DOI: 10.4324/9781003110361-10

Moreover, reasonable defenders might say that in pairing Donald Trump with notorious leaders and ideas of the past, as we have done in this volume, we have exposed ourselves as supporters or members of an insidious American oligarchy.[4] Trump's defenders commonly claim that America's oligarchic elites—a coalition of political, economic, media, and university intellectuals and bureaucrats—are obsessed with destroying Trump from the beginning. Trump directly challenged this ruling elite, depicting them to his faithful as their—and their country's—enemy. If this indictment is valid, then the authors in this volume are at best misguided, or more likely members of that very elite set on destroying Trump as a threat to its power.

We speak in defense of the authors here. They have researched, thought, and written in this volume in the spirit of intellectual honesty and not conspiratorial hate for Trump. All human observers suffer from bias and ignorance, and neither Trump's defenders nor are we immune to these problems. As the chapters here demonstrate, this volume goes beyond Trump and his persona. Through the parallels explored here, this volume serves to argue that some familiar populist and authoritarian traits and actions of past leaders have found a recrudescence in Donald Trump. Yet each of our authors also brings to light that the nature and meaning of Trump's presidency are nuanced. In the end, the reader must decide what to make of the historic parallels, of Donald Trump himself and of his significance for the American democratic project.

Unlike the sharply delineated way that Plutarch constructed his work—Athens to Rome, individual by individual—the parallels to Trump in this volume are historically eclectic and wide-ranging, drawing on a variety of scholarly disciplines and on antiquity, modernity, American history, Maoism, and fascism. Let us look back briefly at the chapters. We began with Mallory Monaco Caterine's look at Plutarch's *Parallel Lives*, the inspiration for this volume. Plutarch used historical comparison of Greek and Roman political figures as a kind of practical pedagogy, helping readers use the past to make sense of the present. The chapter closed by considering Plutarch's enduring influence on American political thought and biography.

Our second chapter sought to make sense of the phenomenon of Trump by looking at the historic starting point, the early Greek city-states, some of them democratic—and, as part of their political development, their critiques of democracy, focused especially on the problem of the demagogue, whose ability to rise to power through popular assent was seen as the critical weakness of the democratic *polis*. As Mark A. Menaldo described in his chapter, "The Politics of Anger: Donald Trump and Cleon of Athens," Cleon typified the ancient demagogue. Menaldo argued that Cleon and Trump were remarkably similar, both before and during their political careers. Both established themselves as bold, boastful, and ill-mannered men; for both, this flouting of conventional niceties and decorum played to their advantage, enabling them to paint themselves as strong-minded, creative disruptors. Overall, Menaldo noted, Trump's political program echoed that of Cleon: angry, fault-finding, and punitive. Like Cleon, Trump broke with a long-standing leadership tradition, which was to avoid unseemliness. In the political communities before the rise of Cleon and of Trump, the people tended to view politicians as elites. As a condition of gaining power, the common expectation was that those elites present themselves as decent men (and women, more recently) of good character who deserved to occupy their office. Cleon in his day, and Trump in his, flipped this script and embraced a new compact with the people by abandoning the established decorum of Athens's Pynx Hill and America's presidential podium. Impulsive, loud, and gifted at direct communication with the people, Cleon helped write the populist playbook that Trump followed so skillfully.

Our third author, Alfonso Vergaray, explored the psychological roots of Trump's demagogic character by comparing him to another ancient model—a type rather than an individual. Vergaray's chapter, "Plato's Tyrannical Soul and Donald Trump's (In)authentic Leadership," examined Plato's analysis of the defects of democracy and the unrestrained tyrannical soul in *The Republic*. Platonic psychology offers an analytic couch on which Vergaray lays Trump's disordered soul. Due to Trump's so nakedly exhibiting his ruling passion—a desire to do as he pleases, without constraint by custom, rule, or counsel—his followers have consistently misinterpreted his words and actions as authentic leadership. This desire for unbridled freedom, Vergaray pointed out, is a common feature of the tyrannical soul, which seeks to free itself of the constraints that most people accept. The consequence of this extreme individual will to freedom, however, is severe. To remain "free," Plato's tyrant must enervate the wills of those around him, especially people who try to restrain his behavior. According to the logic of tyranny, the tyrant must take the whole community hostage (much the same perspective informs Arthur Koestler's lightly fictionalized exploration of Stalin's impact on society, and a true believer, in *Darkness at Noon*). At the same time, though, and in keeping with much of the analysis in our chapters, Vergaray was careful to distinguish true tyranny from Trump's tyrant-like—or tyrant-light—behavior. Indeed, Trump's insurrectionist gambit on January 6 points to two somewhat contradictory and yet both-true conclusions: first, the outgoing President was eager to hold onto power through what was, in effect, an attempted coup (or, to be more precise, a self-coup or *autogolpe*); second, that this was a half-hearted effort, not backed by anything like the full power a sitting President could have brought to the effort. In the contradiction between Trump's wish and his execution, Vergaray located Trump's imperfectly tyrannical soul. Repairing Trump's disordered psychic life is out of the question. But what can be done? Vergaray recommends that society help temper tyrant-like passions in the people through a rededication to civic equality and unity.

Trump's political career has always depended upon his being a creature of theater, of splendid improvisation, careful deployment of slogans and images, and careful cultivation of a particular and familiar image—the strong and vigorous man. To those who are not his fans, the effort put into crafting this image, from the spray tan to the put-on scowl to the jutting jaw, makes the theatrical Trump an inescapable part of his identity. Indeed, it is likely that even among his fans, Trump's allure includes an appreciation of his theatrical flair. Trump's theatrical instincts remind us of Queen Elizabeth I's statement to Parliament (according to the chronicler Holinshed): "We princes . . . are set on stages, in the sight and in view of all the world." Trump has been remarkably good at using lies to represent himself as a simple honest man saying simple true things, as Michael Harvey noted in his chapter, "Politics as Theater: Trump and Machiavelli's Political Actors." Known in his lifetime for his comedy, *La Mandragola*, Machiavelli understood politics as an exercise of theatrics, or the careful management of appearances. Harvey described Machiavelli's astute and nuanced insights about the theatrics of politics in his *Prince* and *The History of Florence*. Harvey's jaunt through many of Machiavelli's examples demonstrates that the Florentine thinker did not think all political actors are created equal. This fact is especially pronounced in two 14-century Florentine strong men: Walter, styled as the Duke of Athens, and the commoner Michele di Lando. While all politics depends on the performance of political actors, performance, and theatricality are not an adequate foundation for political power. Machiavellian politics depends on a deeply ingrained desire to deceive others and hide one's true self. At the same time, such a person must possess sufficient *virtù* that there seems to be no difference between the political man and the role. Trump lacks such virtuosity, but he has managed to remain visible despite his electoral loss by occupying the Republican party's center stage. Indeed, as Harvey suggested, it is possible that Trump's reshaping of the theatrical role, so that the gap between the player and the play becomes visible, is part of how his contemporary audience appreciates him and is drawn to him: a self-consciously ironic, meme-drenched, can't-fool-me-but-I-choose-what-to-believe aspect of the contemporary American citizen.

Trump's literary diet does not include ancient Greek histories of philosophy, or early modern political thought. He sticks to what he (thinks he) knows. His is a blinkered understanding of American history, and his favorite theme is a simple invocation of old-primer-book patriotism and its heroes. As Jason Opal explored in his chapter, "Populism From Above: Donald Trump, Andrew Jackson, and the Politics of White Vengeance," Trump claimed to be the reincarnation of President Andrew Jackson. Jackson laid the American foundations for Trump's anti-establishment candidacy. Known as "Old Hickory," Jackson proved his mettle to the American public by showing extreme hostility to indigenous nations and rebellious slaves. He rode the wave of the ordinary (white) man into power, oversaw the ethnic cleansing of American Indians, and took on American institutions such as the Electoral College and the Second Bank of the United States. Close to two centuries later, Trump's presentation similarly resonated with a white demographic under threat—in Trump's case, more pure decline, with an embittered non-elite white population that saw broken political and economic structures limiting its wealth, family stability, and generational mobility. But while Trump consciously borrowed from the playbook of the immensely popular Jackson, Opal reminds us that Trump remains deeply unpopular in this present political context. Critically, Trump's populist tactics seem to be constrained by the need to sow division, not meaningful unity.

No one, not even his strongest defenders, would call Donald Trump a man of outstanding character. In the contest of discovering flamboyant personalities, however, "The Donald" is an ideal fit. In the early 20th century, society shifted from a concern for character (or its hypocritical performance, at least) to locating and showering attention on striking personalities. This change, from a culture of character to one of personality, was captured by Simonetta Falasca-Zamponi in her chapter, "Idols of Consumption: From Mussolini to Trump." She argued that society's desire to consume the mundane charms of ordinary people turned politicians into performers. Benito Mussolini was one of the earliest examples of a person capitalizing on stardom for the sake of launching his political career. The massive cultural shift in Mussolini's time, in which being someone of importance was equal to merely being somebody, allowed him to rise to power on fame alone. The obsolescence of praise and blame that people once attributed to moral actions was replaced with the reverence of flashy personality descriptors. Americans too were captivated by Mussolini, describing him as "forceful," "attractive," "magnetic," and "energetic." Key to Mussolini's personality was his projection of an extraordinary person amidst the smallness of ordinary followers. The fawning attentiveness of Mussolini's followers helped make him a celebrity. It is this concept—celebrity—that Falasca-Zamponi suggests is the true core of Trump's appeal to his followers. Thus he is in a sense immune to criticisms of weak, fickle, dishonest, or ineffective leadership: in the calculus of celebrity, what matters is attention, not achievement. How stable such a calculus is, and what sort of legacy such a leader leaves, remain to be seen—considering the case of Mussolini and Italy, it is evident that even after such a leader falls, his memory can persist, and cast a shadow for a long time.

Comparing Donald Trump, popularly elected and serving a single four-year term before losing his bid for reelection, and Mao Zedong, who ruled China autocratically for decades, might point to more differences than similarities. But Bin Song, in his chapter comparing these two figures, described an essential parallel: both Mao and Trump relied on, as their chief base of support, personal allegiance from millions of fervent followers who saw themselves engaged in a titanic struggle against elites who had weakened and betrayed the nation, and would do so again if they gained power. This mass of citizens—peasants for Mao, "red-staters" for Trump—saw the two men as avatars of the true nation: strong, heroic men defending a great community's cultural integrity and heritage against faceless bureaucrats and opportunistic political elites. But Song took this populist analysis one step further: beyond cultivating an intensely political loyalty to a hero defending a beleaguered cultural identity, Mao and Trump made an explicitly religious appeal: anti-intellectualism with a religious dimension, or "heart knowledge," as Song translates from the Chinese. Trump, Song argued consistently preferred to appeal to religious belief over bureaucratic or scientific claims of expertise, for instance, in his handling of the Covid-19 pandemic. Neither Mao nor Trump was personally deeply religious, Song concluded but both deftly deployed religious tropes—in the case of Mao, Ruism or Confucian wisdom, and in the case of Trump, biblical allusions.

From Mao, it is a short step to the American president who wove a strategic rapprochement with Mao's China, Richard Nixon. Nixon, a restless thinker and political creature, was at home in the realpolitik logic of reaching out to China while simultaneously appealing to the atavistic racist instincts of white Americans. Nixon's coded racism exploited the cultural divisions of the 1960s and the Vietnam War. As Sarah Thelen explained in her chapter, "From Dog Whistles to Fog Horns: Richard Nixon, Donald Trump, and Their Silent Majorities," Trump's racial politics recommitted to Nixon's "southern strategy." Nixon rallied white support during his administration by coining the term, "The Silent Majority." He used this clever phrase to speak for and to most Americans who supported the Vietnam War and his presidency but did not actively demonstrate their politics. By doing so, Nixon recast dissenters of the Vietnam War's as the fringe while kindling enthusiasm and supporting "grass-roots" (quiet) patriotism among his supporters. But the silence was sometimes broken. In 1970, in New York, a group of pro-Nixon construction workers, predominantly the same non-college-educated whites who would later form the legions of Trump supporters, roared into the streets. They brutalized young students protesting Nixon's invasion of Cambodia and the massacre at Kent State University, days after the Ohio National Guard killed students. Thelen argued that Trump's angle on Nixon's strategy depended on a more intense courtship of white supporters and an encouragement of their willingness to take direct action. Trump stoked feelings of fear and white anger at the growing diversity in American society and politics. Given the bleak political endgame for white nationalism, due to the ever-shrinking number of white voters, Trump ramped up vitriolic rhetoric for his reelection in 2020, as he desperately sought to either pluck more conservative white voters, or throw out ballots altogether.

***

In this second part of our conclusion, we take a more direct view of Trump and his impact on American democracy. Our aim is not only to assess the damage done to American society—which we think is grave—but also to leave our readers with a measure of hope. Trump is both a contributing factor to and a consequence of

American decadence. Trump has done his best to knock down one of the bulwarks of sustainable democracy, a belief in shared civic or political truths and institutions and a confidence that their value and validity endure even in the heat of political contestation. But against even the possibility of shared truths and trusted institutions, Trump's main communicative theme has been to assert fraud and treachery on the part of his political opponents and collusion by the media in that fraud and treachery. Here, for instance, is how Trump spoke about truth and falsehood in his speech to supporters gathered in front of the White House on January 6, 2021, shortly before the storming of the Capitol:

> And you know what else? We don't have a free and fair press. Our media is not free, it's not fair. It suppresses thought, it suppresses speech and it's become the enemy of the people. It's become the enemy of the people. It's the biggest problem we have in this country.

Trump's fierce and persistent communicative efforts to sow mistrust and erode shared civic understanding have served to insulate him, to some extent, from the normal consequences of journalistic investigation—a clever tactic. Beyond that, however, Trump's attack on journalistic and institutional integrity—bad faith everywhere!—has a longer-term effect. Trump has taught a significant group of Americans to believe alternative facts, to distrust information provided by existing institutions, and to create non-factual narratives of fraud and treachery arrayed against his partisans. During the California gubernatorial recall campaign of 2021, for instance, the website for the leading Republican candidate, Larry Elder, urged those visiting the page to "sign a petition to stop the fraud of the California recall election," without specifying any particular fraudulent actions, and even though most fraud allegations concern the counting of votes *after* the election.[5]

Trump's impact on people's ability to think clearly—or their willingness to be misled—calls to mind what Francis Bacon called the "Idols of the Mind," or fallacies that interfere with people's ability to think clearly. Bacon used the term "idols" to connote appealing but false concepts that lodged in the brain and are understood as important truths. Bacon identified four such idols: Idols of the Tribe, or the mental biases inherent to the functioning of human thinking and judging; Idols of the Cave, or the biases each individual develops by virtue of their particular position, occupation, and interest; Idols of the Theater, or old dogma and beliefs accepted by faith or custom; and Idols of the Marketplace, or the chaotic use of words, slogans, labels, and messaging in everyday public and political discourse. In this framework, Trump is a master peddler of "idols of the marketplace," appealing but misleading claims and assertions shaped and delivered through speeches, public statements, and above all thousands of tweets.

Bacon thought that the light of reason, powered by philosophy and science, tended toward the triumph of truth over his four idols. The rise of Trump and Trumpism challenges that optimism. We turn to Bacon's ideas at the end, here, but in the spirit of this volume, use a Plutarchian-inspired analysis to diagnose the chronic disease that is Trumpism. We use an ancient, modern, and post-modern parallel. We contend with society's moral descent, the atrophy of political courage that happens in republics, and the drift into Nietzschean-like nihilism.

Trump's trampling of decorum and appropriateness helped accustom his partisans to a rejection of all manner of values supportive of democratic governance, including stability and trust. Trump acted as the Roman emperor Nero did, beneath his station in a manner that people, for a while at least, found entertaining. The character of Trimalchio of Satyricon (written during Nero's reign) helps convey the sense of descent and decadence that Trump has wrought.[6] Trimalchio comes from the rabble, a freedman who continues to be a slave to wealth and passions. He fancies himself a thinker and poet. Confused about God, he pours libations to himself. Trimalchio holds his guests captive during a feast; no one is free to talk to their neighbors. Only when he relieves himself do the dinner guests have an opportunity to speak freely. The popularity of Trump's Trimalchian feast of tweets and speeches, peppered with accusations, lies, and narcissistic ramblings, suggests how deep American culture has been diminished.

The critical (passive) onlookers are not free of blame. It was their (our) mistake to see Trump as a mere spectacle, a carnival barker. These onlookers were willing to wait it out. Many of us thought that the strength of American political institutions, and the patient and stabilizing resistance of a hostile political bureaucracy, might restrain him. Perhaps that has proved, ultimately, to be the case. But this essentially passive approach comes with risks; the rejection of Trump's challenge to his 2020 electoral loss depended on a few state overseers of electoral integrity refusing to bend to pressure from Trump and his agents. Even a national leader like Mike Pence, Trump's vice-president, the individual charged with certifying the election results, frantically sought to find a middle path between patriotic duty and fealty to Trump. In December, as Pence came under intense pressure to repudiate the national election results from Trump, he called a former Vice-President, Dan Quayle, for counsel. Pence was desperate to find a way to placate Trump. "You don't know the position I'm in," he told Quayle. For his part, Trump, in his January 6 speech shortly before the storming of the Capitol, made a final appeal to his vice-president:

> Because if Mike Pence does the right thing, we win the election. All he has to do, all this is, this is from the number one, or certainly one of the top, Constitutional lawyers in our country. He has the absolute right to do it. We're supposed to protect our country, support our country, support our Constitution, and protect our constitution.
>
> States want to revote. The states got defrauded. They were given false information. They voted on it. Now they want to recertify. They want

it back. All Vice President Pence has to do is send it back to the states to recertify and we become president and you are the happiest people.

And I actually, I just spoke to Mike. I said: "Mike, that doesn't take courage. What takes courage is to do nothing. That takes courage." And then we're stuck with a president who lost the election by a lot and we have to live with that for four more years. We're just not going to let that happen.[7]

As Machiavelli warned us in the 16th century, even states with the best laws may fall prey to internal dissension, conspiracy, and tumult. It came down to the people rejecting Trump in a reelection bid as the last critical defense of American democracy—and his challenge to the system may take more vigorous and effective form in the next presidential election, in 2024.

Indeed, millions of Americans still follow and adore this man, and as of this writing he looms over the Republican party, which has been reshaped in his image—truculent, vindictive, suspicious, promising revelation and triumph just around the corner. Nothing less than a Nietzchean diagnosis fits our situation. There were subterranean scents that Trump detected, the *ressentiment* of his followers. He disdained even a slight concession that there is a common good requiring compromise, but he lacked the zealotry or discipline to wage a sustained ideological campaign: what emerges is a Nietzschean blend of resentment, caprice, and improvisation. Trump's Make America Great Again banner was a nostalgic and vengeful political project. He understood that as the American political parties lost their strength, it was better to seek out enemies rather than friends. As Nietzsche said about the German Reich, "only in opposition does it become necessary." Trump's vision of America, and his role in leading it, relied on such opposition.

We are in a post-Trump administration, but the idolatry of Trump has not died down. The little Trump sycophants now ape him. High on recklessness and low on substance, they sow doubts and spread misinformation. No one can be trusted: elections, news, data, public officials, journalists, doctors, and educators.

There is no quick fix to this problem. Although, as Francis Bacon recognized long ago, nothing is more valuable to the human species than knowledge, there is no appetite among millions of Trump's followers for its patient pursuit: they prefer the instant revelation of Facebook posts touting revelations and conspiracies.[8] We live thus in the world Bacon saw, of the idols of the mind that impede clear thinking. As we have suggested, Bacon's third idol, the idol of the marketplace, is especially pertinent to the phenomenon of Donald Trump. Public discourse is a tangled and confusing undertaking, made up of minds ill fit for the precision of words and definition that deliberation and logic require. What would Bacon have thought of our information sharing in the internet age, which allows for a mass congregation and sharing of peoples' enthusiasms and emotional reactions?

What effect does the character of this new civic space reality have on public discourse and reasoning? Today, everyone seems to only agree to the particular fact that there is no truth. It is not uncommon to deem all information and sources as biased. Many people look upon mainstream media sources and public officials with suspicion and as operatives of shadowy and conspiratorial forces. And as recently as 2017, even higher education in the United States was seen to do more harm than good among conservatives and independents.[9] It takes no great leap of the imagination to speculate that the Covid-19 pandemic and the 2020 US presidential election have made this partisan notion worse. Declining trust in public institutions, including higher education, puts us, teachers and scholars, in a difficult position.

Nevertheless, an overwhelming number of Americans see a college education as a worthwhile investment. Our problem as educators is not that we talk too much about the value of education—but that we say too little. Liberal educators, such as ourselves, have the opportunity and responsibility to grow the spark of curiosity into sustained discipline of the mind. The recipe is simple: show students what study looks like and how to do it themselves. "Student" comes from the Latin *studium*, meaning zealous and painstaking application to a task. Students today are no less curious, no less full of zeal, than in the past. Young people are eager to learn, but now we are virtually born with handheld devices that provide an endless dopamine fix of experiences, images, memes, jokes, snatches of conversation, games, and more. If we want the next generation to fall back in love with the truth, we need to help them slow down, from an onslaught of information in bite-size posts to ideas and facts in their full context. The cultivation of patience and humility are key—beginning with patience and humility in our own role as teachers (and examples).

The university classroom is the special and almost sacred (in a secular sense) space in which so many young people enter and encounter serious study for the first time. We, the authors, attest to this in our own lives. Beginning with an interest in experience, novelty, and change, we began to explore the deeper roots of making sense of the world. These explorations were transformational to our sense of self. We learned the courage to ask questions and dared to stake our identities on new ideas. Such a student develops desires to know things profoundly and broadly. A liberally educated person, in the fullest expression of the liberal ideal, becomes civically inclined and accepts a civic responsibility to protect and improve, in our case, the American republic. The process is slow and delicate because it depends on cultivating concrete ideas that speak to a unique person. This type of schooling has existed for thousands of years. Education is not a panacea to our current ills, but societies have relied on educated and responsible leaders, and citizens, to guide us from time immemorial. It is the responsibility of educators to presume that these future leaders may be populating our classroom. Thus, we have a co-equal responsibility as our students proceed through their formal studies, and especially as they move from college to society, from learning to civic identity and action. We bear the torch of our intellectual predecessors: *sapere aude*, "dare to know."

In the end, if we have not changed the opinions of many of Trump's defenders, then we challenge them to write their parallels of the presidency of Donald Trump. Can it be done, except as a satire? Could anyone write a good book in praise of the Inquisition?[10] If such parallels can teach us something of value, then, by all means, reasonable Trump defenders lead the way.[11]

Notes

1 We refer here to various conservative voices that have stridently defended Trump in such venues as the, The Claremont Institute, and its publication *American Mind,* and another publication called, *American Greatness.*

2 David Hanson, "Trump Winds and Biden Whirlwinds," *American Greatness*, July 11, 2021, https://amgreatness.com/2021/07/11/trump-winds-and-biden-whirlwinds/.

3 De Cive, 1642, Ch. 3, Sec. 31.

4 Angelo Codevilla, "American Exodus," *Tablet*, March 24, 2021.

5 Elise Viebeck and Tom Hamburger, "Trump, Elder's Campaign Falsely Claimed Fraud Before California Votes Were Counted—A Growing GOP Tactic," *Washington Post*, September 15, 2021, www.washingtonpost.com/politics/2021/09/15/trump-elder-california-recall-fraud-newsom/.

6 See Petronius Arbiter, *Satyricon*, Cena Trimalchionis (Banquet of Trimalchio), ch. 26–78.

7 Hayes Brown, "Dan Quayle Talked Mike Pence into Rejecting Trump," *MSNBC*, September 17, 2021, www.msnbc.com/opinion/dan-quayle-talked-mike-pence-rejecting-trump-what-story-n1279406.

8 See Francis Bacon, *Novum Organum* (New York: P.F. Collier, 1902).

9 www.pewresearch.org/politics/2017/07/10/sharp-partisan-divisions-in-views-of-national-institutions/.

10 See George Orwell, "The Prevention of Literature," in *Shooting an Elephant and Other Essays* (London: Secker and Warburg, 1950).

11 Victor David Hanson's *The Case for Trump* (2019) makes a case for Trump as a "tragic hero"—an uncouth, norm-breaking Western cowboy who has taken on the thankless job of doing the nation's dirty work. Hanson compares Trump to General George S. Patton, Dirty Harry, and the Greek hero Ajax. In our opinion, this is not Hanson's best work.

INDEX

Note: Page numbers followed by "n" indicate a note on the corresponding page.

For Product Safety Concerns and Information please contact our EU representative GPSR@taylorandfrancis.com
Taylor & Francis Verlag GmbH, Kaufingerstraße 24, 80331 München, Germany

www.ingramcontent.com/pod-product-compliance
Ingram Content Group UK Ltd.
Pitfield, Milton Keynes, MK11 3LW, UK
UKHW022018180926
475701UK00005B/908

* 9 7 8 0 3 6 7 6 2 6 9 5 2 *